Ukulele Chord Songbook

ISBN 978-1-4803-2131-1

7777 W. BLUEMOUND RD. P.O. BOX 13819 MILWAUKEE, WI 53213

For all works contained herein:
Unauthorized copying, arranging, adapting, recording, Internet posting, public performance,
or other distribution of the printed music in this publication is an infringement of copyright.
Infringers are liable under the law.

Visit Hal Leonard Online at
www.halleonard.com

Ukulele Chord Songbook

Contents

The A Team

Words and Music by
Ed Sheeran

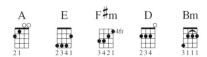

A	E	F#m	D	Bm

Intro |A | E |F#m   D |A |

Verse 1

    A
    White lips, pale face

           E   **F#m**
Breathin' in snow - flakes,

       D   **A**
Burnt lungs, sour taste.

Lights gone, day's end,

          E   **F#m**
Struggling to pay ____ rent

     D   **A**
Long nights, strange men.

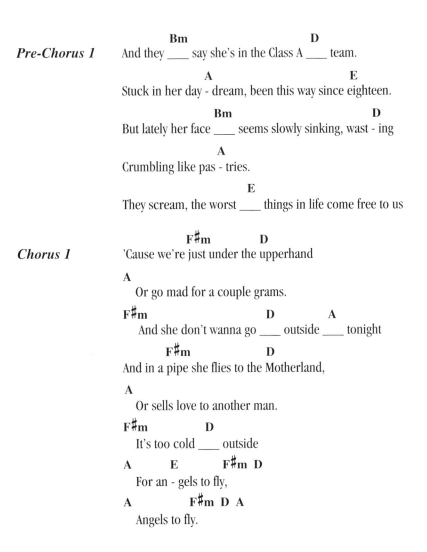

Pre-Chorus 1

         Bm   **D**
And they ___ say she's in the Class A ___ team.

              A   **E**
Stuck in her day - dream, been this way since eighteen.

           Bm   **D**
But lately her face ___ seems slowly sinking, wast - ing

            A
Crumbling like pas - tries.

                E
They scream, the worst ___ things in life come free to us

Chorus 1

       F♯m   **D**
'Cause we're just under the upperhand

A
  Or go mad for a couple grams.

F♯m   **D**   **A**
  And she don't wanna go ___ outside ___ tonight

     F♯m   **D**
And in a pipe she flies to the Motherland,

A
  Or sells love to another man.

F♯m   **D**
  It's too cold ___ outside

A   **E**   **F♯m D**
  For an - gels to fly,

A   **F♯m D A**
  Angels to fly.

Verse 2

        A
Ripped gloves, raincoat

              E   **F♯m**
Tried to swim to stay ____ afloat,

            E   **A**
Dry house, wet clothes.

Loose change, bank notes,

            E   **F♯m**
Weary eyed, dry throat,

          E   **A**
Cool girl, no phone.

Pre-Chorus 2

            Bm   **D**
And they ____ say she's in the Class A ____ team.

              A   **E**
Stuck in her day - dream, been this way since eighteen.

                 Bm   **D**
But lately her face ____ seems slowly sinking, wast - ing

              A
Crumbling like pas - tries.

                         E
And they scream, the worst ____ things in life come free to us

Chorus 2

         F♯m   **D**
'Cause we're just under the upperhand

A
  Or go mad for a couple grams.

F♯m   **D**   **A**
  And she don't wanna go ____ outside ____ tonight

         F♯m   **D**
And in a pipe she flies to the Motherland,

A
  Or sells love to another man.

F♯m   **D**
  It's too cold ____ outside

A   **E**
  For an - gels to fly.

Bridge

            Bm   D   F♯m
An angel will die covered in white

              A
Closed eyed and hoping for a better life

      Bm   D
This ____ time we'll fade out to - night

                 F♯m D A F♯m D A
Straight down the line.

Pre-Chorus 3

        Bm   D
They ____ say she's in the Class A ____ team.

           A   E
Stuck in her day - dream, been this way since eighteen.

             Bm   D
But lately her face ____ seems slowly sinking, wast - ing

              A
Crumbling like pas - tries.

                E
They scream, the worst ____ things in life come free to us

Chorus 3

         F♯m   D
And we're all under the upperhand

A
  Go mad for a couple grams.

F♯m   D   A
  We don't wanna go ____ outside ____ tonight

       F♯m   D
And in the pipe we fly to the Motherland,

A
  Or sell love to another man.

F♯m   D
  It's too cold ____ outside

A   E   F♯m D
  For an - gels to fly,

A   F♯m D A
  Angels to fly.

     F♯m   D A
To fly, ____ fly.

              F♯m   D   A
For angels to fly, ____ to fly, ____ to fly.

E   A
Angels to die.

Blow Me (One Last Kiss)

Words and Music by
Alecia Moore and Greg Kurstin

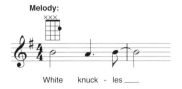

Melody:

White knuck - les ___

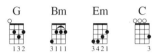

G	Bm	Em	C

Intro |G | Bm |Em | C |

Verse 1

      G   Bm   Em
White knuckles   and sweaty palms

                C
From hanging on ___ too tight.

G   Bm
Clenched, shut jaw,

Em   C
I've got another headache again ___ tonight.

G   Bm
  Eyes on fire, eyes on fire, and the burn

                    Em
From all the tears ___ I've been cry'n', I've been cry'n',

          C
I've been dy - in' over you.

G   Bm
  Tie a knot in the rope, try'n' to hold, ___ try'n' to hold,

Em   N.C.
  But there's nothing to grab so I ___ let go.

Chorus 1

	G		Bm
	I think I've fin'lly had enough,	I think I maybe think too much.	

Em   C
I think this might be it for us. Blow me one last kiss.

G   Bm
You think I'm just too serious,   I think you're full of shit.

Em   C
My head is spinning, so blow me one last kiss.

G   Bm
Just when it can't get worse, ____ I've had a shit day.

Em   C
Have you had a shit day?   We've had a shit day.

G
I think that life's too short for this,

Bm
Want back my ignorance and bliss.

Em   C   G
I think I've had enough of this. Blow me one last kiss.

Verse 2

G   Bm Em   C
I won't miss   all the fighting that we al - ways did.

G   Bm Em   C
Take it in,   I mean what I say when I say there is noth - ing left.

G   Bm
No more sick whiskey dick, no more bat - tles for me.

Em   C
You'll be calling a trick, 'cause you'll no ____ longer sleep.

G   Bm
I'll dress nice, I'll look good, I'll go danc - ing alone.

Em   N.C.
I will laugh, I'll get drunk, I'll take some - body home.

		G		Bm	

Chorus 2

      G   **Bm**
I think I've fin'lly had enough,   I think I maybe think too much.

  Em   **C**
I think this might be it for us. Blow me one last kiss.

  G   **Bm**
You think I'm just too serious,   I think you're full of shit.

  Em   **C**
My head is spinning, so blow me one last kiss.

G   **Bm**
Just when it can't get worse, ____ I've had a shit day.

  Em   **C**
Have you had a shit day?   We've had a shit day.

  G
I think that life's too short for this,

  Bm
Want back my ignorance and bliss.

  Em   **C**   **G**
I think I've had enough of this. Blow me one last kiss.

G   **Bm**   **Em** **C**
La, la, la, la, la, la, la, la. ____ Blow me one last kiss.

G   **Bm**   **Em** **C**
La, la, la, la, la, la, la, la. ____ Blow me one last kiss.

Bridge 1

  G   **Bm**
I will do what I please, anything ____ that I want.

  Em   **C**
I will breathe, I will breathe, I won't wor - ry at all.

  G   **Bm**
You will pay for your sins, you'll be sor - ry, my dear.

  Em   **N.C.**
All the lies, all the whys will all be crystal clear.

Chorus 3   *Repeat Chorus 1*

Bridge 2
     G
‖:   Na, na, na, na, na, na, na, na.

Bm
  Na, na, na, na, na, na, na, na.

Em
  Na, na, na, na, na, na, na, na.

C
Blow me one last kiss. :‖

Outro
  G   **Bm**
Just when it can't get worse, ____ I've had a shit day.

Em   **C**
  Have you had a shit day?   We've had a shit day.

G
  I think that life's too short for this,

Bm
  Want back my ignorance and bliss.

Em   **C**   **G**
  I think I've had enough of this. Blow me one last kiss.

Born This Way

Words and Music by
Stefani Germanotta, Jeppe Laursen,
Paul Blair and Fernando Garibay

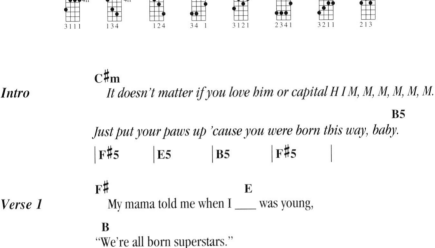

Intro

C#m
It doesn't matter if you love him or capital H I M, M, M, M, M, M.

B5
Just put your paws up 'cause you were born this way, baby.

| F#5 | E5 | B5 | F#5 | |

Verse 1

F#   E
My mama told me when I ___ was young,

B
"We're all born superstars."

F#   E
She rolled my hair put my lipstick on

B
In the glass of her boudoir.

F#   E
"There's nothin' wrong with lovin' who you are,"

            B
She said, "'cause He made you perfect, babe.

F#   E
So hold your head up, girl, and you'll go far."

B   N.C.
Listen to me when I say…

Chorus 1	F# E I'm beauti - ful in my way, 'cause God makes no mistakes.

Chorus 1

                        F#   E
I'm beauti - ful in my way, 'cause God makes no mistakes.
             B   F#
I'm on the right track, baby. I was born this way.

                                          E
Don't hide yourself in regret, just love your - self and you're set.
             B   F#
I'm on the right track, baby. I was born this way.
                          E
Ooh, there ain't no other way. Baby, I was born this way.
B   F#
Baby, I was born this way, ___ born this way.
                          E
Ooh, there ain't no other way. Baby, I was born this way.
B   F#
Right track, baby, I was born this way.

Interlude

             N.C.
Don't be a drag, just be a queen.

Don't be a drag, just be a queen.

Don't be a drag, just be a queen.

Verse 2

N.C.
Give yourself prudence and love your friends,
                             B
Subway kid, rejoice the truth.
F#   E
   In the religion of the insecure
         B
I must be myself, respect my youth.
F#   E
   A diff'rent lover is not a sin,
         B
Believe capital H I M.
F#   E
   I love my life, I love this record,
        B
And mi amore vole fe yah.

Chorus 2

Repeat Chorus 1

Bridge   ‖: C#m | :‖

      C#m
Don't be a drag, just be a queen,

Whether you're broke or evergreen.

You're black, white, beige, chola descent,
                            N.C.
You're Lebanese, you're orient.
     F#5
Wheth - er life's disabilities left you outcast, bullied or teased,

Rejoice and love yourself today 'cause baby, you were born this way.
        F#   E
No matter gay, straight or bi, lesbian transgendered life,
        B   F#
I'm on the right track, baby. I was born to survive.
                                 E
No matter black, white or beige, chola or orient made,
        B   F#
I'm on the right track. Baby, I was born to be brave.

Chorus 3

         F#   E
I'm beauti - ful in my way, 'cause God makes no mistakes.

        B   F#
I'm on the right track, baby. I was born this way.

                          E
Don't hide yourself in regret, just love your - self and you're set.

        B   F#
I'm on the right track, baby. I was born this way.

                   E
Ooh, there ain't no other way. Baby, I was born this way.

B   F#
Baby, I was born this way, ___ born this way.

                   E
Ooh, there ain't no other way. Baby, I was born this way.

B   F#
Right track, baby, I was born this way.

                 E
I was born this way, hey, I was born this way, hey.

        B   F#
I'm on the right track, baby. I was born this way, hey.

        N.C.
I was born this way, hey, I was born this way, hey.

I'm on the right track, baby. I was born this way, hey.

Outro

  F#   F#m F#   F#m
‖: *Same D.N.A.*   *but born this way.*   :‖

Breakeven

Words and Music by Stephen Kipner,
Andrew Frampton, Daniel O'Donoghue
and Mark Sheehan

I'm still a - live but I'm bare - ly breath - in',

Ebmaj7   Bb   Fsus4   Gm7   Gm   Cm7   F

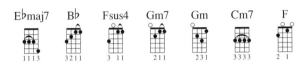

Intro

```
||: Ebmaj7   Bb   |Fsus4   Gm7          |
|Ebmaj7   Bb   |Fsus4   Gm7          :||
|Gm      Fsus4   |Bb      Cm7          |
```

Verse 1

> Gm   Fsus4   Bb Cm7
> I'm still alive but I'm barely breathin',
>
>   Gm   Fsus4   Bb Cm7
> Just prayin' to a God that I don't believe in.
>
>   Gm   Fsus4   Bb Cm7
> 'Cause I got time while she got freedom.
>
>   Gm   Fsus4   Bb Cm7
> 'Cause when a heart breaks, no, it don't break even.

Verse 2

Gm   Fsus4   B♭ Cm7
Her best days will be some of my worst.

Gm   Fsus4   B♭   Cm7
She fin'lly met a man that's gonna put her first.

     Gm   Fsus4   B♭ Cm7
While I'm wide awake, she's no trouble sleep - in'.

     Gm   Fsus4   B♭   Cm7
'Cause when a heart breaks, no, it don't break even, ___ even, ___ no.

Chorus 1

E♭maj7   B♭
What am ___ I s'posed to do

        F   Gm7
When the best part of me was always you,

    E♭maj7   B♭
And   what am ___ I s'posed to say

        F   Gm7
When I'm all choked up that you're okay?

E♭maj7 B♭   F Gm7 E♭maj7
   I'm fallin' to piec - es, yeah.

B♭   F Gm7 Gm Fsus4 B♭ Cm7
I'm fallin' to piec - es.

Verse 3

     Gm   Fsus4   B♭ Cm7
They say bad things happen for a reason,

     Gm   Fsus4   B♭ Cm7
But no wise word's gonna stop the bleedin'.

      Gm   Fsus4   B♭ Cm7
'Cause she's moved on while I'm still grievin',

     Gm   Fsus4   B♭   Cm7
And when a heart breaks, no, it don't break even, ___ even, ___ no.

Chorus 2

E♭maj7   B♭
And what am ____ I gonna do

      F   Gm7
When the best part of me was always you,

   E♭maj7   B♭
And   what am ____ I s'posed to say

       F   Gm7
When I'm all choked up that you're okay?

E♭maj7 B♭   F Gm7   E♭maj7
    I'm fallin' to piec - es, yeah.

B♭   F Gm7 E♭maj7
I'm fallin' to piec - es,   yeah.

B♭   F Gm7 E♭maj7
I'm fallin' to piec   - es,

B♭   F Gm7
I'm fallin' to piec - es.

‖: Gm   F |B♭   E♭maj7 :‖

Bridge

          Gm   F
Oh, you've got his heart and my heart and none of the pain.

B♭   E♭maj7
You took your suit - case, I took the blame.

       Gm   F   B♭ E♭maj7
Now I'm try'n' to make sense of what little remains, ____ oh.

'Cause you left me with no love and no love to my name.

Verse 4

Gm   Fsus4   B♭ Cm7
  I'm still alive but I'm barely breathin',

    Gm   Fsus4   B♭ Cm7
Just prayin' to a God that I don't believe in.

      Gm   Fsus4   B♭ Cm7
'Cause I got time while she got freedom.

       Gm   Fsus4
'Cause when a heart breaks, no, it don't break,

B♭   Cm7   E♭maj7
No, it don't break, no, it don't break even.

Chorus 3

            B♭
What am ___ I gonna do

         F   **Gm7**
When the best part of me was always you,

    E♭maj7   **B♭**
And   what am ___ I s'posed to say

         F   **Gm7**
When I'm all choked up that you're okay?

E♭maj7 B♭   **F Gm7**   **E♭maj7**
     I'm fallin' to piec - es, yeah.

B♭   **F Gm7 E♭maj7**
I'm fallin' to piec - es,   yeah.

B♭   **F Gm7 E♭maj7**
I'm fallin' to piec   -   es,

B♭   **F Gm7**   **E♭maj7 B♭ F Gm7**
I'm fallin' to piec - es,

E♭maj7 B♭ F Gm7   **E♭maj7 B♭**
          Oh, it don't break e   - ven, no.

Fsus4 Gm7   **E♭maj7 B♭**
    Oh, it don't break e -   ven, no.

Fsus4 Gm7   **E♭maj7 B♭**   **Fsus4 Gm7**
    Oh, it don't break e -   ven, no.

Outro   ‖: **E♭maj7 B♭** | **Fsus4   Gm7**   :‖ *Repeat and fade*

Drive By

Words and Music by Pat Monahan,
Espen Lind and Amund Bjorklund

Melody:

On the oth-er side of a street I knew

C#m A E B F#m G#7sus4 G#7 G#m7 G# Aadd9

Intro |C#m | |

Verse 1

     C#m
On the other side of a street I knew

     A
Stood a girl that looked like you.

    E   **B**
I guess that's a déjà vu, but   I thought this can't be true

        C#m   **A**
'Cause   you moved to west L.A. or   New York or Santa Fe

      E   **B**
Or   wherever to get away from ____ me.

Pre-Chorus 1

F#m   **A**
Oh, but that one night   was more than just right.

C#m   **B**
I didn't leave you   'cause I was all through.

F#m   **A**
Oh, I was overwhelmed   and frankly scared as hell

G#7sus4   **G#7**
Because I really fell ____ for you.

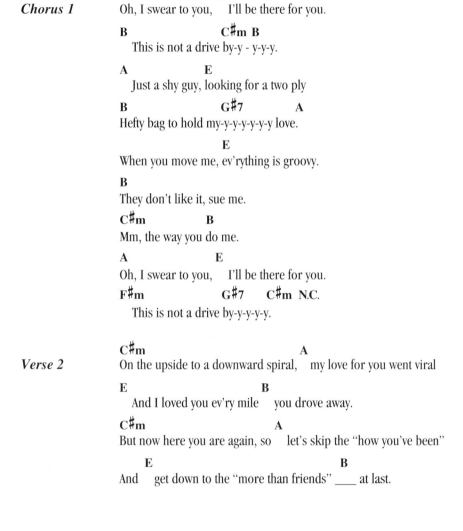

Chorus 1

A   E
Oh, I swear to you, I'll be there for you.

B   C♯m B
 This is not a drive by-y - y-y-y.

A   E
 Just a shy guy, looking for a two ply

B   G♯7   A
Hefty bag to hold my-y-y-y-y-y-y love.

        E
When you move me, ev'rything is groovy.

B
They don't like it, sue me.

C♯m   B
Mm, the way you do me.

A   E
Oh, I swear to you, I'll be there for you.

F♯m   G♯7 C♯m N.C.
 This is not a drive by-y-y-y-y.

Verse 2

C♯m   A
On the upside to a downward spiral, my love for you went viral

E   B
 And I loved you ev'ry mile you drove away.

C♯m   A
But now here you are again, so let's skip the "how you've been"

    E   B
And get down to the "more than friends" ____ at last.

Pre-Chorus 2

F#m   A
Oh, but that one night   is still the highlight.

C#m   B
  I didn't need you   until I came to.

F#m   A
  And I was overwhelmed   and frankly scared as hell

G#7sus4   G#7
  Because I really fell ___ for you.

Chorus 2

A   E
Oh, I swear to you,   I'll be there for you.

B   C#m B
  This is not a drive by-y - y-y-y.

A   E
  Just a shy guy, looking for a two ply

B   G#7   A
Hefty bag to hold my-y-y-y-y-y love.

                 E
When you move me, ev'rything is groovy.

B
They don't like it, sue me.

C#m   B
Mm, the way you do me.

A   E
Oh, I swear to you,   I'll be there for you.

F#m   G#7
  This is not a drive by-y-y-y-y.

Bridge

G#m7   C#m   F#m   B
Please believe ___ that when I leave

      G#   F#m   B
There's nothin' up my sleeve ___ but love for you

And a little time to get my head together, too.

Verse 3

C#m
On the other side of the street I knew

A
Stood a girl that looked like you.

E   B   N.C.
I guess that's déjà vu, but   I thought this can't be true ____ 'cause

Chorus 3

A   E
Oh, I swear to you,   I'll be there for you.

B   C#m B
This is not a drive by-y - y-y-y.

A   E
Just a shy guy, looking for a two ply

B   G#7   A
Hefty bag to hold my-y-y-y-y-y-y love.

                            E
When you move me, ev'rything is groovy.

B
They don't like it, sue me.

C#m   B
Mm, the way you do me.

A   E
Oh, I swear to you,   I'll be there for you.

F#m   G#7   Aadd9
This is not a drive by-y-y-y-y.

Forget You

Words and Music by Bruno Mars,
Ari Levine, Philip Lawrence,
Thomas Callaway and Brody Brown

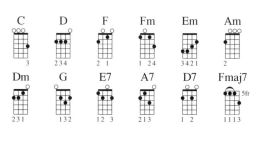

Intro C| D| F| C|

Chorus 1

         C   **D**
I see you drive 'round town with the girl I love,

     F   **C**
And I'm like, forget you.

                      D
I guess the change in my pocket ____ wasn't enough.

 F   **C**
I'm like, forget you and forget her, too.

             D   **F**
Said if I was richer,   I'd still be wit' ya.

                    C
Ha, now ain't that some shit?   (Ain't that some shit?)

And although there's pain in my chest,

 D   **F**   **Fm** **C**
I still wish you the best with a forget you.

Verse 1

               C   D
Yeah, I'm sorry   I can't afford a Ferrari,

                  F   C
But that don't mean I can't get you there.

                                         D
I guess he's an Xbox and I more an Atari,

                  F
But the way you play your game ain't fair.

C   D
   I pity the fool that falls in love with you.

     F
(Oh, shit, she's a gold digger.)

                C
Well, (Just thought you should know nigga.)

                      D
Ooh, I've got some news for you, ha, ha.

F   C
Yeah, go and run and tell your little boyfriend.

Chorus 2   *Repeat Chorus 1*

                    C   D

Verse 2   Now I know   that I had to borrow,

                  F   C
Beg and steal and lie and cheat

                                     D
Tryin' to keep ya, tryin' to please ya.

                       F   C
'Cause being in love ___ with your ass ain't cheap.

                             D
I pity the fool that falls in love with you, oh, oh.

     F
(Oh, shit, she's a gold digger.)

                C
Well. (Just thought you should know nigga.)

                      D
Ooh, I've got some news for you, ha, ha.

           F   C
Ooh,   I'm gonna hate your ass   right now.

Chorus 3   *Repeat Chorus 1*

　　　　　　　　　　Em　　　　　　　　　　　　Am
Bridge   Now, baby, baby, baby, why do you wanna,

　　　　　　　　　　　　　　　Dm
Wanna hurt me so bad?

　　　　　　　　　　　　　G
(So bad, so bad, ____ so bad.)

　　　　　　　　　　Em　　　　　E7　　　　　　Am
I tried to tell my mama, but she told me,

　　　　　　　　　G　　Am　　A7　　　　D7
"This is one for your dad."

　　　　　　　　　　　　　　　G
(Your dad.) Yes, ____ she did. (Your dad.)

　　　　　　　　　　　　　D7　N.C.　　　F　N.C.　　　Fmaj7　N.C.
And I'm like (Uh,)　 why, (uh,)　 why, (uh.)　　　　　　 why,

　　　　　　　　　Am　G　　Am　　A7　　D7　N.C.
La - dy? _____ (Oh.)

　　　　　　　　　　　　　Fmaj7　N.C.　　　　G
I love you,　(Oh,)　 I still love you, oh.

　　　　　　　　　　　　　C　　　　　　　　　　D
Outro-Chorus   I see you drivin' 'round town with the girl I love,

　　　　　　　　　F　　　　　C
Oh, forget you.

　　　　　　　　　　　　　　　　　　　D
I guess the change in my pocket ____ wasn't enough.

　　　　　　　　　　F　　　　　　　　　C
I'm like, forget you and forget her, too.

　　　　　　　　　　　　　D　　　　　　　　F
Said if I was richer, I'd still be wit' ya.

　　　　　　　　　　　　　　　C
Ha, now ain't that some shit?　　(Ain't that some shit?)

And although there's pain in my chest,

　　　　　　　　　D　　　　　　　　　　　F　　Fm　C
I still wish you the best with a forget you.

Ho Hey

Words and Music by
Jeremy Fraites and Wesley Schultz

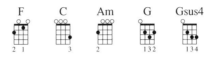

Intro

  F C F C F

‖:   (Ho! Hey!) :‖

Verse 1

C   **F**
(Ho!) I've been try'n' to do it right.

C   **F**
(Hey!) I've been living a lonely life.

C   **F**
(Ho!) I've been sleeping here instead,

C
(Hey!) I've been sleeping in my bed,

Am   **G F**
(Ho!) I've been sleeping in my bed.

C **F C F**
(Hey! Ho!)

Verse 2

C   **F**
(Ho!) So show me, family,

C   **F**
(Hey!) All the blood that I will bleed.

C   **F**
(Ho!) I don't know where I belong,

C
(Hey!) I don't know where I went wrong,

Am   **G** **F** **C**
(Ho!) But I can write a song. ___ (Hey!)

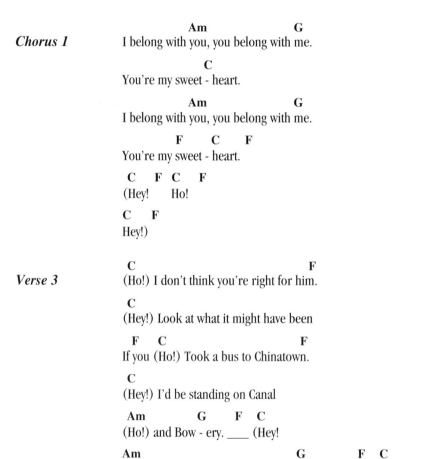

Chorus 1

     Am   **G**
I belong with you, you belong with me.

       C
You're my sweet - heart.

     Am   **G**
I belong with you, you belong with me.

     F **C** **F**
You're my sweet - heart.

 C **F** **C** **F**
(Hey! Ho!

 C **F**
Hey!)

Verse 3

 C   **F**
(Ho!) I don't think you're right for him.

 C
(Hey!) Look at what it might have been

 F **C**   **F**
If you (Ho!) Took a bus to Chinatown.

 C
(Hey!) I'd be standing on Canal

 Am   **G** **F** **C**
(Ho!) and Bow - ery. ____ (Hey!

 Am   **G**   **F** **C**
Ho!) You should be standing next ____ to me. ____ (Hey!)

Chorus 2

                           Am   **G**

‖: I belong with you, you belong with me,

                   C

You're my sweet - heart. :‖

Bridge

         F **C**   **Gsus4**

And love ____ we need ____ it now.

C   **F**   **C**   **Gsus4**

 Let's hope, ____ let's hope for some,

           F **C**   **Gsus4**   **C**

'Cause oh, ____ we're bleeding out.

Outro-Chorus

                  Am   **G**

I belong with you, you belong with me,

               C

You're my sweet - heart.

                  Am   **G**

I belong with you, you belong with me,

           F   **C**   **F**

You're my sweet - heart.

 C   **F** **C**   **F**

(Hey!   Ho!

C

Hey!)

Gangnam Style

Words and Music by
Gun Hyung Yoo and Jai Sang Park

Op-pan Gang-nam style   Gang-nam style

Bm   Em   F#m   G   A   B   F#

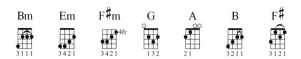

Intro | N.C.(Bm) | | | |

Oppan Gangnam style

| | | | | Em   F#m |

Gangnam style

N.C.(Bm)

Verse 1 *Najeneun tasaroon inganjeogin yeoja*

Keopi hanjane yeoyureur aneun

Poomgyeok inneun yeoja

Bami omyeon shimjangi tuegeowojineun yeoja

Geureon banjeon inneun yeoja.

Em F#m   N.C.(Bm)
        Naneun sanai Najeneun neomankeum tasaroun geureon sanai

Keopi shikgido jeone wonshat taerineun sanai

                                                                  Em F#m
Bami omyeon shimjangi teojeobeorineun sanai Geureun sana - i.

Chorus 1

         G   **A**   **B**
Areum - dawo sarangseu - reowo Geurae neo *hey*

Geurae baro neo *hey*

         G   **A**
Areum - dawo sarangseu - reowo
     F♯
Geurae neo hey geurae baro neo *hey*

Jigeumbooteo galdekaji gabolka?
N.C.   **(Bm)**
  Oppan Gangnam style Ah

Gangnam style Op-op-op-op

Oppan Gangnam style Ah

Gangnam style Op-op-op-op
Em   **F♯m**
  Oppan Gangnam style.
N.C.(Bm)
Eh sexy lady *Op-op-op-op*

Oppan Gangnam style

Eh sexy lady *Op-op-op-op*
Em   **F♯m**
Eh-eh-eh-eh-eh-eh

Verse 2

N.C.(Bm)
Jeongsookkae boijiman nol taen noneun yeoja

Itaedashipeumyeon mookeotteon meori pooneun yeoja

Garyeotjiman wenmanhan nochoolboda yahan yeoja

Geureron gamgakjeogin yeoja

Em F#m   N.C.(Bm)
      Naneun sanai Jeomjana boijiman nol taen noneun sanai

Taega dwemyeon wanjeon michyeobeorineun sanai

Geunyookboda sasangiooltoongbooltoonghan sanai

          Em F#m
Geureon sana - i

Chorus 2   *Repeat Chorus 1*

Bridge

N.C.(Bm)
Twineun nom Geu wie naneun nom

Baby baby Naneun mwor jom aneun nom

Twineun nom Geu wie naneun nom

Baby baby Naneun mwor jom aneun nom

                              You know what I'm sayin'?

Outro

N.C.
   Oppan Gangnam style

Em   F#m   N.C.(Bm)
Eh-eh-eh-eh-eh-eh-eh

Sexy lady, *Op-op-op-op oppan Gangnam style.*

Eh sexy lady *Op-op-op-op*

Em   F#m   N.C.   Bm
Eh-eh-eh-eh-eh-eh   *Oppan Gangnam style Ah.*

English Translation

Intro

Oppa lives a Gangnam style life

Gangnam style

Verse 1

(I love) a lady who is warm and compassionate by the day

A classy lady who can afford a relaxing cup of coffee

But whose heart starts burning when the night comes

A lady who has such a twisted charm

I'm a guy

A guy who is as warm as you by the day

A guy who downs the boiling hot coffee one go

A guy whose heart starts exploding when the night comes

I'm that kind of guy.

Chorus

Beautiful, lovely, yes you are, hey, yes you are hey

Beautiful, lovely, yes you are, hey, yes you are, hey

Shall we go all the way from now on?

Oppa lives a Gangnam style life

Eh, sexy lady, oppa lives a Gangnam style life.

Verse 2

(I love) a virtuous lady who can have a ball

A lady who undoes her ponytail when the time comes

And who's sexy even without wearing skimpy clothes

Such a sensuous lady

I'm a guy

A guy who goes completely crazy when the time comes

And whose ideas are bumpier than his muscles

I'm that kind of guy.

Bridge

Over a running guy, there's a flying guy

Baby, baby, I'm kind of a know it all

You know what I'm sayin'?

Oppa lives a Gangnam style life

Eh, sexy lady, oppa lives a Gangnam style life.

Good Life

Words and Music by Ryan Tedder,
Eddie Fisher, Brent Kutzle and
Noel Zancanella

Woke up   in Lon - don yes - ter-day, ____

G   C   Em   D

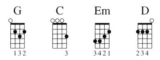

132	3	3421	234

Intro   ‖: G |C |Em |D   :‖

Verse 1

      G   **C**
Woke up in London yesterday,

                                   Em
Found myself in the city near Picca - dilly.

                     D
Don't really know how I got ____ here,

                       G
I got some pictures on my phone.

                              C
New names and numbers that I don't know,

                      Em
Address to places like Abbey Road.

                              D
Day turns to night, night turns to what - ever we want.

We're young enough to say...

Chorus 1

```
G                              C
Oh, this has gotta be the good ___ life.

                      Em
This has gotta be the good ___ life.

                      D
This could really be a good ___ life, good life.

    G                              C
I say oh, got this feelin' that you can't ___ fight,

                  Em
Like this city is on fire ___ tonight.

                      D
This could really be a good ___ life, a good, good life.

 G   C  Em  D
(Oh, oh, oh.)
```

Verse 2

```
G                                  C
  To my friends in New York, I say hel - lo.

                      Em
My friends in L.A., they don't know

                          D
Where I've been for the past few years or so,

       N.C.            G
Paris to China to Colorad - o.

                          C
Sometimes there's airplanes I can't jump out.

                          Em
Sometimes there's bullshit that don't work now.

                      D
We all got our stories. But please, tell me what there's to complain about.
G                          C              Em
  When you're happy like a fool, ___ let it take you o - ver.

                  D
When ev'rything is out, ___ you gotta take it in.
```

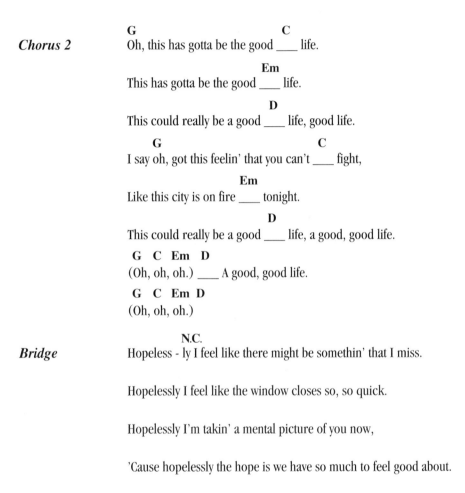

Chorus 2

  G   C
Oh, this has gotta be the good ___ life.

                             Em
This has gotta be the good ___ life.

                                D
This could really be a good ___ life, good life.

    G   C
I say oh, got this feelin' that you can't ___ fight,

                           Em
Like this city is on fire ___ tonight.

                                D
This could really be a good ___ life, a good, good life.

  G C Em D
(Oh, oh, oh.) ___ A good, good life.

  G C Em D
(Oh, oh, oh.)

Bridge

                        N.C.
Hopeless - ly I feel like there might be somethin' that I miss.

Hopelessly I feel like the window closes so, so quick.

Hopelessly I'm takin' a mental picture of you now,

'Cause hopelessly the hope is we have so much to feel good about.

Chorus 3   *Repeat Chorus 2*

Verse 3

        G   **C**
To my friends in New York, I say hel - lo.

                         Em
My friends in L.A., they don't know

                             D
Where I've been for the past few years or so,

                  G
Paris to China to Colorad - o.

                         C
Sometimes there's airplanes I can't jump out.

                           Em
Sometimes there's bullshit that don't work now.

                      D **N.C.**
We all got our stories. But please, tell me what there's to complain about.

Outro   ‖: N.C.(G) | :‖ ***Repeat and fade***

Good Time

Words and Music by Adam Young,
Matthew Thiessen and Brian Lee

Melody:

Ab6 Eb Bb Cm Ab

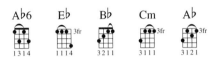

Verse 1

       Ab6 Eb Bb Cm
           Ha,

       Ab6   Eb   Bb
        Whoa, ___ oh.

           Cm
       It's always a good time.

       Ab6   Eb   Bb
        Whoa, ___ oh.

           Cm   **Ab6 Eb Bb N.C.**
       It's always a good time, babe.

Verse 2

       Ab6   Eb   Bb   Cm
        Woke ___ up on the right side ___ of the bed.

       Ab6   Eb   Bb   Cm
        What's up with this Prince song inside my head?

       Ab6   Eb   Bb   Cm
        Hands ___ up if you're down to get down tonight.

       Ab6 Eb Bb   **N.C.**
        'Cause it's always a good time.

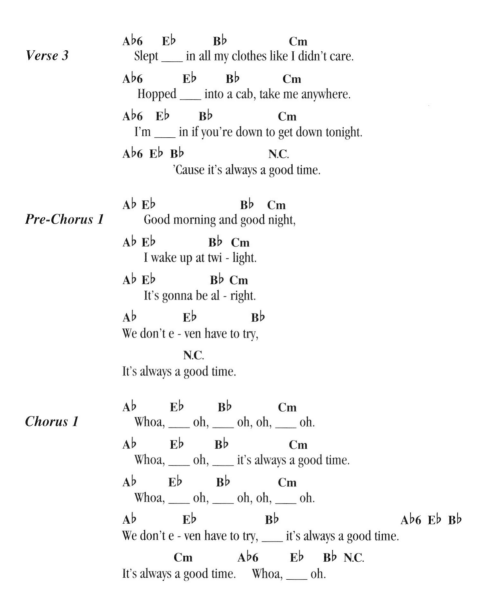

Verse 3

A♭6   E♭   B♭   Cm
Slept ___ in all my clothes like I didn't care.

A♭6   E♭   B♭   Cm
Hopped ___ into a cab, take me anywhere.

A♭6   E♭   B♭   Cm
I'm ___ in if you're down to get down tonight.

A♭6 E♭ B♭   N.C.
'Cause it's always a good time.

Pre-Chorus 1

A♭ E♭   B♭ Cm
Good morning and good night,

A♭ E♭   B♭ Cm
I wake up at twi - light.

A♭ E♭   B♭ Cm
It's gonna be al - right.

A♭   E♭   B♭
We don't e - ven have to try,

              N.C.
It's always a good time.

Chorus 1

A♭   E♭   B♭   Cm
Whoa, ___ oh, ___ oh, oh, ___ oh.

A♭   E♭   B♭   Cm
Whoa, ___ oh, ___ it's always a good time.

A♭   E♭   B♭   Cm
Whoa, ___ oh, ___ oh, oh, ___ oh.

A♭   E♭   B♭   A♭6 E♭ B♭
We don't e - ven have to try, ___ it's always a good time.

              Cm   A♭6   E♭   B♭ N.C.
It's always a good time.   Whoa, ___ oh.

Verse 4

A♭6   E♭   Bb   Cm
Freaked ___ out, dropped my phone in the pool again.

A♭6   E♭   B♭   Cm
Checked out of my room, hit the ATM.

A♭6   E♭   B♭   Cm
Let's hang ___ out if you're down to get down tonight.

A♭6 E♭ B♭   N.C.
'Cause it's always a good time.

Pre-Chorus 2   *Repeat Pre-Chorus 1*

Chorus 2

A♭   E♭   B♭   Cm
Whoa, ___ oh, ___ oh, oh, ___ oh.

A♭   E♭   B♭   Cm
Whoa, ___ oh, ___ it's always a good time.

A♭   E♭   B♭   Cm
Whoa, ___ oh, ___ oh, oh, ___ oh.

A♭   E♭   B♭
We don't e - ven have to try, ___ it's always a good time.

A♭   E♭   B♭   Cm
Whoa, ___ oh, ___ oh, oh, ___ oh.

A♭   E♭   B♭   Cm
Whoa, ___ oh, ___ it's always a good time.

A♭   E♭   B♭   Cm
Whoa, ___ oh, ___ oh, oh, ___ oh.

A♭   E♭   B♭
We don't e - ven have to try, ___ it's always a good time.

A♭   E♭ B♭   Cm
Doesn't matter when, it's always a good time then.

A♭   E♭ B♭   Cm
Doesn't matter where, it's always a good time there.

A♭   E♭ B♭   Cm
Doesn't matter when, it's always a good time then.

A♭ E♭ B♭
It's always a good time.

Chorus 3

A♭   E♭   B♭   Cm
Whoa, ___ oh, ___ oh, oh, ___ oh.

A♭   E♭   B♭   Cm
Whoa, ___ oh, ___ it's always a good time.

A♭   E♭   B♭   Cm
Whoa, ___ oh, ___ oh, oh, ___ oh.

A♭   E♭   B♭
We don't e - ven have to try, ___ it's always a good time.

A♭   E♭   B♭   Cm
Whoa, ___ oh, ___ oh, oh, ___ oh.

A♭ E♭   B♭   Cm
Whoa, ___ oh, ___ it's always a good time.

A♭   E♭   B♭   Cm
Whoa, ___ oh, ___ oh, oh, ___ oh.

A♭   E♭   B♭
We don't e - ven have to try, ___ it's always a good time.

Outro-Chorus

A♭6   E♭   B♭   Cm
‖: Whoa, ___ oh, ___ oh, oh, ___ oh.

A♭6   E♭   B♭   Cm
Whoa, ___ oh, ___ it's always a good time. :‖ ***Repeat and fade***

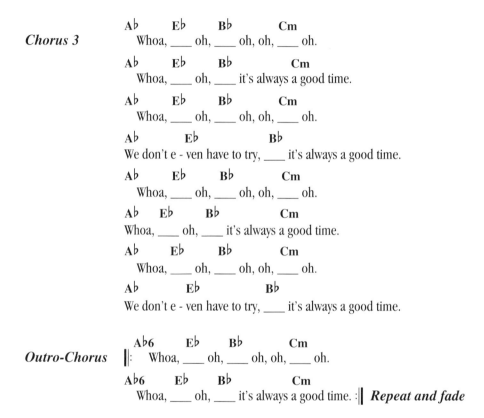

Home

Words and Music by
Greg Holden and Drew Pearson

Melody:

Hold on _____ to me

C   Csus4   Csus4   Am7   F   Cmaj7   Am   G   Gsus4

Intro

‖: C | | Csus4 | :‖

Verse

     C   Csus4   C   Csus4
Hold on ___ to me as we go,

          C   Csus4   C   Csus4
As we roll down ___ this unfamiliar road.

               Am7 F   C   Csus4
And although this wave ___ is stringing us along,

      C   Cmaj7 F C Am
Just know you're not alone,

              C   G   C
'Cause I'm gonna make this place your ___ home.

Chorus 1

   C   Csus4   C   Csus4
Settle down, ___ it'll all be ___ clear.

   C   Csus4
Don't pay no mind to the demons,

         C   Csus4
They fill you with fear.

Am7   F
Trouble, it might drag you down.

       C   G
You get lost, you can always be found.

      C   G   Am G Am
Just know you're not a - lone,

          F   C G   C
'Cause I'm gonna make this place your ___ home.

Bridge 1	|F Ooh,	|	|C	|	|

	|F Ooh,		|C		
	|Am Ooh.		|G		
	|F Ooh.		|C	|G	
	|		|Gsus4	|G	

	|:F Oh,		|C		
	|Am Oh.		|G		
	|F Oh.		|C	|G	
	|		|Gsus4	|G	:|

Chorus 2 *Repeat Chorus 1*

Bridge 2

	|:F Oh,		|C		
	|Am Oh.		|G		
	|F Oh.		|C	|G	
	|		|Gsus4	|G	:|

Outro

	|F Oh,		|C		
	|Am Oh.		|G		
	|F Oh.		|C	|G	|

It's Time

Words and Music by Daniel Reynolds,
Benjamin McKee and Daniel Sermon

Melody:

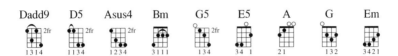

So   this   is   what _ you   meant _

| Dadd9 | D5 | Asus4 | Bm | G5 | E5 | A | G | Em |

Intro ‖: N.C.(Dadd9) | : ‖

Verse 1

D5
So this is what you meant when you said that you were spent.

Asus4
And now it's time to build from the bottom of the pit

Bm
Right to the top.

Don't hold back.

G5   **D5**
Packing my bags, and giving the Academy a rain - check.

Pre-Chorus 1

D5   **Asus4**
I don't ever wanna let you down.

Bm
I don't ever wanna leave this town.

G5
'Cause after all, ____ this city never sleeps at night.

Chorus 1

D5
It's time to begin, isn't it?

           Bm
I get a little bit bigger, but then, I'll admit,

               E5
I'm just the same as I was.

                         G5
Now, don't you understand, ____ that I'm never changing who I am?

Interlude

| **D5** | | **Asus4** | | |
| **Bm** | | **G5** | | |

Verse 2

G5
So this is where you fell, and I am left to sell.

Asus4
  The path to heaven runs through miles of clouded hell,

          Bm
Right to the top.

Don't look back.

G5   **D5**
  Turning to rags, and giving the commodities a rain - check.

Pre-Chorus 2   *Repeat Pre-Chorus 1*

Chorus 2

        D5
‖: It's time to begin, isn't it?

          Bm
I get a little bit bigger, but then, I'll admit,

             E5
I'm just the same as I was.

                   G5
Now, don't you understand, ____ that I'm never changing who I am? :‖

Bridge
Bm   **A**
   This road never looked so lonely.

                          G
This house doesn't burn down slowly

        Em   **G5**
To ash - es, to ash - es.

Chorus 3
Asus4   **N.C.**
    It's time to begin, isn't it?

I get a little bit bigger, but then, I'll admit,

               E5
I'm just the same as I was.

                  G5
Now don't you understand, ____ that I'm never changing who I am?

     Bm
It's time to begin, isn't it?

            D
I get a little bit bigger, but then, I'll admit,

            G5
I'm just the same as I was.

E5   **G5**   **Asus4**   **D5**
   Now, don't you understand, ____ that I'm never changing who I am?

Jar of Hearts

Words and Music by
Barrett Yeretsian, Christina Perri
and Drew Lawrence

Melody:

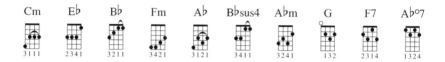

I know I can't take one more ___ step ___ towards ___ you,

Cm	Eb	Bb	Fm	Ab	Bbsus4	Abm	G	F7	Ab°7
3111	2341	3211	3421	3121	3411	3241	132	2314	1324

Verse 1

   Cm   **Eb**
I know I can't take one more ___ step towards you,

  Bb   **Fm**
'Cause all that's waiting is regret.

  Cm   **Eb**
And don't you know I'm not your ___ ghost anymore,

  Bb   **Ab**   **Eb**
You lost the love I loved the most.

Pre-Chorus 1

  Fm   **Ab** **Cm**   **Bb**
I learned to live half a - live

  Fm   **Ab**   **Bbsus4**   **Bb**
And now you want me one more ___ time.

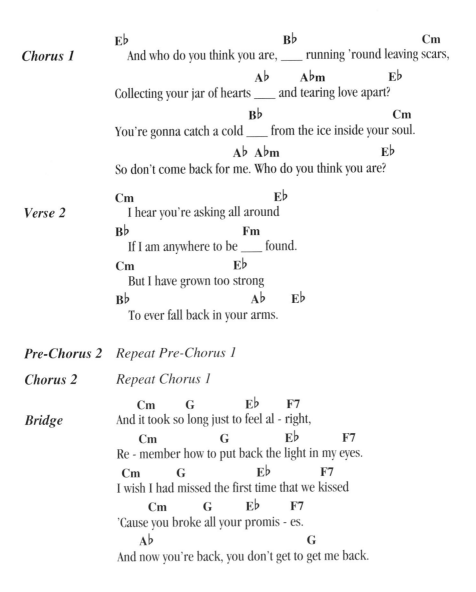

Chorus 1

E♭   B♭   Cm
And who do you think you are, ___ running 'round leaving scars,

                          A♭   A♭m   E♭
Collecting your jar of hearts ___ and tearing love apart?

                    B♭   Cm
You're gonna catch a cold ___ from the ice inside your soul.

                 A♭   A♭m   E♭
So don't come back for me. Who do you think you are?

Verse 2

Cm   E♭
I hear you're asking all around

B♭   Fm
If I am anywhere to be ___ found.

Cm   E♭
But I have grown too strong

B♭   A♭   E♭
To ever fall back in your arms.

Pre-Chorus 2   *Repeat Pre-Chorus 1*

Chorus 2   *Repeat Chorus 1*

Bridge

    Cm   G   E♭   F7
And it took so long just to feel al - right,

    Cm   G   E♭   F7
Re - member how to put back the light in my eyes.

   Cm   G   E♭   F7
I wish I had missed the first time that we kissed

     Cm   G   E♭   F7
'Cause you broke all your promis - es.

   A♭   G
And now you're back, you don't get to get me back.

Chorus 3

Eb   Bb   Cm
And who do you think you are, ___ running 'round leaving scars,

         Ab   Abm   Eb
Collecting your jar of hearts ___ and tearing love apart?

         Bb   Cm
You're gonna catch a cold ___ from the ice inside your soul.

       Ab Abm   Eb
So don't come back for me, don't come back at all.

         Bb   Cm
And who do you think you are, ___ running 'round leaving scars,

         Ab Abm   Eb
Collecting your jar of hearts, ___ tearing love apart?

         Bb   Cm
You're gonna catch a cold ___ from the ice inside your soul.

        Ab Abm   Eb
Don't come back for me,   don't come back at all.

Outro

  Ab°7   Eb
‖: Who do you think you ___ are? :‖

Ab°7   Eb
Who do you think you are?

Just Dance

Words and Music by Stefani Germanotta,
RedOne and Aliaune Thiam

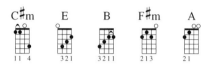

C#m   E   B   F#m   A

Intro

```
|N.C.(C#m) (E)  |(B) (F#m) |C#m E  |B  F#m  |
                                          Red
|C#m   E  |B  F#m   |C#m   E  |B  F#m  |
 One,      Kon - vict, Ga, Ga.     Oh, ___ yeah.
```

Verse 1

```
    C#m      E         B     F#m
     I've had a little bit too much, much.

    C#m      E         B        F#m
     All of the people start to rush. (Start to rush by.)

    C#m      E          B        F#m
     A dizzy twister dance, can't find my drink or man.

    C#m      E          B        F#m
     Where are my keys? I lost my phone, phone.
```

Pre-Chorus 1

```
    A                    C#m
     What's goin' on on the floor?

                                              A
    I love this record, baby, but I can't see straight anymore.

                                   C#m
    Keep it cool. What's the name of this club?

                           N.C.
    I can't remember, but it's alright, al - right.
```

	C#m E B F#m
Chorus 1	Just dance, gonna be okay. Da, da, do, do.

                C#m   E   B   F#m

Just dance, spin that record, babe.   Da, da, do, do.

                C#m   E   B   F#m

Just dance, gonna be okay.   D-d-d-

                   C#m   E   B   F#m   N.C.

Dance, ___ dance, ___ dance, ___ just, ___ just, just, just dance.

	C#m E B F#m
Verse 2	Wish I could shut my playboy mouth.

C#m   E   B   F#m

How'd I turn my shirt inside out? (In - side out, right.)

C#m   E   B   F#m

Control your poison, babe, roses have thorns they say.

C#m   E   B   F#m

And we're all gettin' hosed to - night.

Pre-Chorus 2	*Repeat Pre-Chorus 1*

	C#m E B F#m
Chorus 2	Just dance, gonna be okay. Da, da, do, do.

                C#m   E   B   F#m

Just dance, spin that record, babe.   Da, da, do, do.

                C#m   E   B   F#m

Just dance, gonna be okay.   D-d-d-

                  C#m   E   B   F#m

Dance, ___ dance, ___ dance, ___ just, ___ just, just, just...

Verse 3

C#m E   B   F#m

When I come through on the dance floor, checking out that catalog,

C#m E   B   F#m

Can't be - lieve my eyes, so many women without a flaw.

C#m E   B   F#m

And I ain't gon' give it up, steady try'n' to pick it up like a call.

C#m E   B   F#m

I'm a hit it up, a beat it up, latch on to it until tomorrow.

Pre-Chorus 3

A   C#m

Shawty, I can see that you got so much energy,

                A

The way you twirling up them hips 'round and 'round.

                C#m

And there is no reason at all why you can't leave here with me.

                N.C.

In the meantime stay and let me watch you break it down and...

Chorus 3

C#m   E   B   F#m

Dance, gonna be okay. Da, da, do, do.

 C#m   E   B   F#m

Just dance, spin that record, babe. Da, da, do, do.

 C#m   E   B   F#m

Just dance, gonna be okay. Da, da, do, do.

 C#m   E   B   F#m

Just dance, spin that record, babe. Da, da, do, do.

 C#m   E   B F#m

Just dance, gonna be okay. D-d-d

  C#m   E   B   F#m   C#m

Dance, ___ dance, ___ dance, ___ just, ___ just, just, just dance.

Bridge

N.C.(C♯m)

Amazing music! Wooh! Let's go!

                               (B)   **(C♯m)**

‖: Half psychotic, sick hypnot - ic, got my blueprint, it's symphon - ic.

                         (B)   **(C♯m)**

Half psychotic, sick hypnot - ic, got my blueprint electron - ic.   :‖

            (B)   **(C♯m)**

Go, use your muscle, carve it out, work it, hus - tle.

                (B)   **(C♯m)**

(I got it, just stay close enough to get it.) Don't slow!

        (B)   **(C♯m)**

Drive it, clean it lysol, bleed it, spend the last dough

               (B)

(I got it.) In your pocko! (I got it.)

Chorus 4

        C♯m   E   B   F♯m

‖: Just dance, gonna be okay.   Da, da, do, do.

        C♯m   E   B   F♯m

Just dance, spin that record, babe.   Da, da, do, do. :‖

        C♯m   E   B   F♯m

Just dance, gonna be okay.   D-d-d-

        C♯m   E   B   F♯m   N.C.

Dance, ___ dance, ___ dance, ___ just, ___ just, just, just dance.

The Lazy Song

Words and Music by Bruno Mars,
Ari Levine, Philip Lawrence and
Keinan Warsame

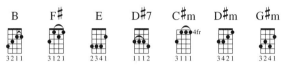

B	F♯	E	D♯7	C♯m	D♯m	G♯m
3 2 1 1	3 1 2 1	2 3 4 1	1 1 1 2	3 1 1 1 (4fr)	3 4 2 1	3 2 4 1

Chorus 1

        B   F♯   E
To - day I don't feel like doin' an - ything.

B   F♯   E
I just wanna lay in my bed.

      B   F♯
Don't feel like pickin' up ____ my phone,

    E
So leave a message at the tone

       B   D♯7   E   N.C.
'Cause to - day I swear I'm not doin' an - ything. Ah.

Verse 1

        B   F♯
I'm gonna kick my feet up then stare at the fan,

E
Turn the TV on, throw my hand in my pants.

B   F♯   E
Nobody's goin' tell me I can't, ____ no.

      B   F♯
I'll be loungin' on the couch just chillin' in my Snuggie,

E
Click to MTV so they can teach me how to dougie.

      B   F♯   E
'Cause in my castle, I'm the frickin' ____ man.

Pre-Chorus 1

    C#m   D#m
Oh, yes, I said it,   I said it.

   E   F#
I said it 'cause I can.

Chorus 2

    B   F#   E
To - day I don't feel like doin' an - ything.

    B   F#   E
I just wanna lay in my bed.

      B   F#
Don't feel like pickin' up ___ my phone,

    E
So leave a message at the tone

        B   D#7   E   N.C.
'Cause to - day I swear I'm not doin' an - ything, noth - in' at all.

Interlude

 B   F#   E   B
 (Woo, hoo,   woo, hoo, hoo.) Nothin' at all.

        F#   E
(Woo, hoo,   woo, hoo, hoo.)

Verse 2

      B   F#
Tomorrow I'll wake up, do some P-Ninety-X,

    E
Meet a really nice girl, have some really nice sex.

   B   F#   E
And she's gonna scream out, "This is great!" __

(Oh my God, this is great.)

    B   F#
Yeah, I might mess around and get my college degree.

  E
I bet my old man will be so proud of me.

   B   F#   E
But sorry, Pops, you'll just have to wait.

Pre-Chorus 2   *Repeat Pre-Chorus 1*

Chorus 3

     B   F♯   E
To - day I don't feel like doin' an - ything.

   B   F♯   E
I just wanna lay in my bed.

        B   F♯
Don't feel like pickin' up ___ my phone,

    E
So leave a message at the tone

         B   D♯7   E
'Cause to - day I swear I'm not doin' an - ything.

Bridge

  N.C. C♯m   F♯
  No, I ain't gonna comb my hair

   G♯m
'Cause I ain't goin' anywhere,

C♯m   F♯   G♯m
No, no, no, no, no, no, no, no, no, oh.

    C♯m   F♯
I'll just strut in my birthday suit

   G♯m
And let ev'rything hang loose,

C♯m   F♯   G♯m
Yeah, yeah, yeah, yeah, yeah, yeah, yeah, yeah, yeah, yeah.

Chorus 4

N.C.   B   F♯   E
  Oh, to - day I don't feel like doin' an - ything.

B   F♯   E
I just wanna lay in my bed.

        B   F♯
Don't feel like pickin' up ___ my phone,

    E
So leave a message at the tone

         B   D♯7   E   N.C.
'Cause to - day I swear I'm not doin' an - ything, noth - in' at all.

Outro

B   F♯   E   B
(Woo, hoo,   woo, hoo, hoo.) Nothin' at all.

        F♯   E   N.C.
(Woo, hoo,   woo, hoo, hoo.) Nothin' at all.

Little Lion Man

Words and Music by
Mumford & Sons

Melody:

Weep for __ your- self, my man, you'll nev - er be __

Dm   F   Fmaj9   Fadd2   B♭maj7sus2   C6sus4   Fsus2   B♭add2

231   2 1   132   3 1   3 4 1   1 3   3 2 1 4

Intro
‖: **Dm** | | **F** | :‖ *Play 4 times*

Verse 1

Dm
Weep for yourself, my man,

                                F
You'll never be what is in your ___ heart.

Dm
Weep, little lion man,

                                    F
You're not as brave as you were at the   start.

Fmaj9
Rate yourself and rake yourself,

Dm   **F**   **Fadd2**   **F**
Take all the courage you have ___ left

     Fmaj9   **Dm**
And wasted on fixing all the problems

                 F   **Fadd2**   **F**
That you made in your own   head.

Chorus 1

           Dm   **B♭maj7sus2** **F**
But it was not your fault but mine,

             Dm   **B♭maj7sus2** **F**
And it was your heart on the   line,

           Dm   **B♭maj7sus2**   **F**
I really fucked it up ____ this time,

              C6sus4
Didn't I my ____ dear? Didn't I my…

Interlude 1   ‖: **Dm** | |**F** | :‖

Verse 2

Dm
Tremble for yourself, my man,

                           F
You know that you have seen this all be - fore.

Dm
Tremble, little lion man,

                   F
You'll never settle any of your ____ scores.

      Fmaj9
Your grace is wasted in your face,

      Dm   **F**   **Fadd2**   **F**
Your boldness stands a - lone a - mong the wreck.

      Fmaj9
Now learn from your mother

      Dm   **F**   **Fadd2**   **F**
Or else spend the days biting _____ your own neck.

Chorus 2

            Dm   **B♭maj7sus2** **F**
‖: But it was not your fault but mine,

             Dm   **B♭maj7sus2** **F**
And it was your heart on the   line,

           Dm   **B♭maj7sus2**   **F**
I really fucked it up ____ this time,

              C6sus4
Didn't I my ____ dear? :‖

Didn't I my dear?

| *Interlude 2* | ‖: Dm   \| \| F   \| :‖ |
| | ‖: Fsus2   \| F   \| B♭add2   \| :‖ |

Bridge

| Fsus2 | F | B♭add2 | |

Ah. _____ Ah. __

| Fsus2 | F | B♭add2 | |

_____ Ah. __

| Fsus2 | F | B♭add2 | |

_____ Ah. __

| Fsus2 | F | B♭add2 | |

_____ Ah.__

| Fsus2 | F | B♭add2 | |

_____ Ah. __

| Fsus2 | F | B♭add2 |

_____ But it was

Chorus 3

Dm N.C.   F
Not your fault but mine,

          Dm   B♭maj7sus2   F
And it was your heart on the   line,

        Dm   B♭maj7sus2   F
I really fucked it up ____ this time,

        C6sus4
Didn't I my ____ dear?

Outro-Chorus

        Dm N.C.
But it was not _____ your fault but mine,

And it was your heart on the line,

I really fucked it up this time,

                C
Didn't I my dear? Didn't I my dear?

Little Talks

Words and Music by
Nanna Hilmarsdottir and
Ragnar Thorhallsson

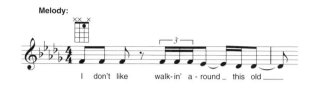

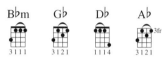

I don't like walk-in' a-round _ this old _____

Bᵇm	Gᵇ	Dᵇ	Aᵇ

Intro

‖: Bᵇm | Gᵇ | Dᵇ | Aᵇ   :‖ *Play 3 times*

Hey!

| Bᵇm | Gᵇ | Dᵇ | Aᵇ |

Verse 1

              Bᵇm   Gᵇ   Dᵇ
Female: I don't like walking around this old ___ and empty house.

            Bᵇm   Gᵇ   Dᵇ
Male: So hold my hand, I'll walk with you my dear.

              Bᵇm   Gᵇ   Dᵇ
Female: The stairs creak as you sleep, it's keep - ing me awake.

              Bᵇm   Gᵇ   Dᵇ
Male: It's the house telling you ___ to close your eyes.

             Bᵇm   Gᵇ   Dᵇ
Female: An' some days I can't even   trust myself.

           Bᵇm   Gᵇ   Dᵇ
Male: It's killing me to see you this way.

Chorus 1

                      Bᵇm   Gᵇ
Both: 'Cause though the truth may vary

         Dᵇ   Aᵇ
This   ship will carry

        Bᵇm Gᵇ   Dᵇ
Our bodies safe to shore.

Interlude 1   *Repeat Intro*

Verse 2	**B♭m** **G♭** **D♭**

                              B♭m   **G♭**   **D♭**

Female: There's an old voice in my head that's   holding me back.

             B♭m   **G♭**   **D♭**

Male: Well, tell her that I miss our little talks.

         B♭m   **G♭**   **D♭**

Female: Soon it will be over and buried with our past.

         B♭m   **G♭**   **D♭**

Male: We used to play out - side when we were young,

And full of life and full of love.

         B♭m   **G♭**   **D♭**

Female: Some days I don't know if I am wrong or right.

         B♭m   **G♭**   **D♭**

Male: Your mind is playing tricks on you, my dear.

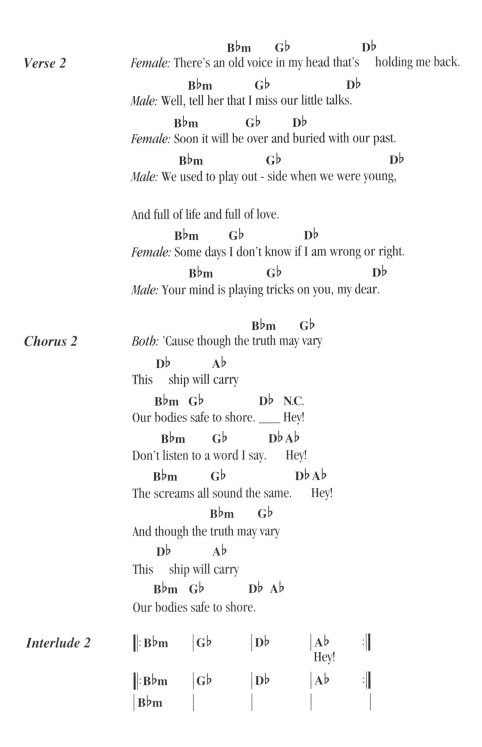

Chorus 2	**B♭m** **G♭**

Both: 'Cause though the truth may vary

      D♭   **A♭**

This   ship will carry

     B♭m **G♭**   **D♭** **N.C.**

Our bodies safe to shore. ___ Hey!

      B♭m   **G♭**   **D♭ A♭**

Don't listen to a word I say.   Hey!

      B♭m   **G♭**   **D♭ A♭**

The screams all sound the same.   Hey!

          B♭m   **G♭**

And though the truth may vary

     D♭   **A♭**

This   ship will carry

     B♭m **G♭**   **D♭ A♭**

Our bodies safe to shore.

Interlude 2	‖: **B♭m** |**G♭** |**D♭** |**A♭** :‖ Hey! ‖: **B♭m** |**G♭** |**D♭** |**A♭** :‖ | **B♭m** | | | |

Verse 3

             B♭m
Both: You're gone, gone, gone away. I watched you disappear.

All that's left is the ghost of you.

Now we're torn, torn, torn apart, there's nothin' we can do.

Just let me go, we'll meet again soon.
  B♭m   G♭   D♭
Now wait, wait, wait for me.   Please hang around.
  B♭m   G♭   D♭ N.C.
I'll see you when I fall asleep. ___ Hey!

Chorus 3

           B♭m   G♭   D♭ A♭
‖: *Both:* Don't listen to a word I say.   Hey!
   B♭m   G♭   D♭ A♭
The screams all sound the same.   Hey!
      B♭m   G♭
And though the truth may vary
   D♭   A♭
This   ship will carry
  B♭m G♭   D♭ A♭
Our bodies safe to shore.   :‖

Outro-Chorus

             B♭m   G♭
Both: And though the truth may vary
   D♭   A♭
This   ship will carry
  B♭m G♭   D♭
Our bodies safe to shore.
      B♭m   G♭
Though the truth may vary
   D♭   A♭
This   ship will carry
  B♭m G♭   D♭
Our bodies safe to shore.

Live While We're Young

Words and Music by Rami Yacoub,
Savan Kotecha and Carl Falk

Melody:

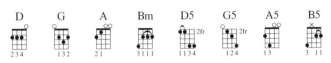

Hey, girl, I'm wait - in' on ya,

D G A Bm D5 G5 A5 B5

Intro

‖: D   G D |N.C.   :‖

Verse 1

      D   G   D
Hey, girl, I'm waitin' on ya,

    G   D
I'm waitin' on ya.

            G   D A
Come on and let me sneak you out,

  D   G   D
And have a celebra - tion,

    G   D
A celebra - tion,

       G   D A
The music up, the win - dows down.

Bm   G   D   A
  Yeah, ___ we'll be doin' what we do,

    Bm   G
Just pretendin' that we're cool,

        A
And we know it, too.

Bm   G   D   A
  Yeah, ___ we'll keep doin' what we do,

    Bm   G
Just pre - tendin' that we're cool.

Chorus 1

      A   N.C.   D5
So to - night,   let's go crazy, crazy,

Bm   G A D
Crazy 'til we see the sun.

  D5   Bm
I know we only met,

            G   A D
But let's pre - tend it's love

  D5   Bm
And never, never, never stop

  G5 A5 B5
For an - y - one.

  D5   Bm
To - night, let's get some

G   A5   D
  And live while we're young.

  A Bm A G   A
Oh, oh, oh, oh, oh, oh, oh.

     D A Bm   G A D
Oh, ___ oh, oh, oh, oh, oh, oh.

     D A Bm A G   A
Oh, ___ oh, oh, oh, oh, oh, oh.

     D   A Bm A
To - night, let's get some

N.C.   D G D N.C.
  And live while we're young

Verse 2

D   G   D
Hey, girl, it's now or nev - er,

  G   D
It's now or nev - er.

          G   D A
Don't over think, just let it go.

D   G   D
And if we get togeth - er,

    G   D
Yeah, get togeth - er,

         G   D A
Don't let the pictures leave the phone.

     Bm   G   D   A
Oh, ___ yeah, ___ we'll be doin' what we do,

        Bm   G
Just pre - tendin' that we're cool.

Chorus 2

       A   **N.C.**   **D5**
So to - night,   let's go crazy, crazy,

Bm   **G** **A** **D**
Crazy 'til we see the sun.

  D5   **Bm**
I know we only met,

          G   **A**   **D**
But let's pre - tend it's love

    D5   **Bm**
And never, never, never stop

    G5 **A5** **B5**
For an - y - one.

    D5   **Bm**
To - night, let's get some

G   **A5**   **D**
   And live while we're young.

    A **Bm** **A** **G**   **A**
Oh, oh, oh, oh, oh, oh, oh.

       D **A** **Bm**   **G** **A** **D**
Oh, ___ oh, oh, oh, oh, oh, oh.

       D **A** **Bm** **A** **G**   **A**
Oh, ___ oh, oh, oh, oh, oh, oh.

       D   **A** **Bm** **A**
To - night, let's get some
N.C.   **D**   **A** **Bm**
   And live while we're young.

Bridge

G   **D** **A**
   And girl, ___ you and I,

Bm   **G**   **D**
   We 'bout to make some memories tonight.

A   **Bm**
I wanna live while we're young.

G   **N.C.**
We wanna live while we're young.

Chorus 3

      D5   **Bm**
Let's go crazy, crazy, crazy

    G A D
'Til we see the sun.

D5   **Bm**
I know we only met,

      G   A D
But let's pre - tend it's love

    D5   **Bm**
And never, never, never stop

  G5 A5 B5
For an - y - one.

     D5   **A**   **Bm A**
To - night, let's get some

G5   **A5**
  And live while we're

D5   **Bm**
Crazy, crazy, crazy

    G A D
'Til we see the sun.

 D5   **Bm**
I know we only met,

      G   A D
But let's pre - tend it's love

   D5   **Bm**
And never, never, never stop

  G5 A5 B5
For an - y - one.

     D5   **A**   **Bm A**
To - night, let's get some
G5   **A5**   **D5**
  And live while we're young.

Outro

     A   Bm A   G
Wanna live, wanna live,

        A   D5
Wan - na live while we're young.

     A   Bm A   G
Wanna live, wanna live,

     A   D
  Wan - na live while we're young.

     A   Bm A   G
Wanna live, wanna live,

        A
Wan - na live while…

         D   A Bm A
To - night, let's get some
N.C.
  And live while we're young.

Moves Like Jagger

Words and Music by Adam Levine,
Benjamin Levin, Ammar Malik and
Johan Schuster

Melody:

Just shoot for the stars ___

Bm7   Em7

4 1 2   2 3 1 4

Intro

| Bm7 | | | | |
| Em7 | | | | |

Verse 1

                                    Bm7
Male: Just shoot for the stars ___ if it feels right.

And aim for my heart if you feel like it.

            Em7
Take me away ___ and make it okay.

I swear I'll behave.

            Bm7
You wanted control ___ so we waited.

I put on a show, now we're naked.

            Em7
You say I'm a kid, ___ my ego is big.

I don't give a shit. And it goes like this.

Chorus 1

        Bm7

Both: Take me by the tongue and I'll know you.

Kiss me 'til you're drunk and I'll show you
        Em7
Male: All the moves like Jagger.

I've got the moves like Jagger.

I've got the moves like Jagger.
        Bm7
Both: I don't need to try to control you.

Look into my eyes and I'll own you
        Em7
Male: With the moves like Jagger.

I've got the moves like Jagger.

I've got the moves like…

Verse 2

        Bm7
Maybe it's hard ____ when you

Feel like you're broken and scarred.

Nothing feels right.
        Em7
But when you're with me ____ I'll make you believe

That I've got the key.
        Bm7
Oh, so get in the car, ____ you can ride it wherever you want.

Get inside it.
        Em7
And you wanna steer ____ but I'm shiftin' gears.

I'll take it from here. Oh, yeah, yeah.

And it goes like this.

Chorus 2

Bm7
Both: Take me by the tongue and I'll know you.

Kiss me 'til you're drunk and I'll show you

Em7
Male: All the moves like Jagger.

I've got the moves like Jagger.

I've got the moves like Jagger.

Bm7
Both: I don't need to try to control you.

Look into my eyes and I'll own you

Em7
Male: With the moves like Jagger.

I've got the moves like Jagger.

I've got the moves like Jagger.

Verse 3

Bm7
Female: Uh, you wanna know how to make me smile?

Take control, own me just for the night.

Em7
But if I share my secret, you're gonna have to keep it.

Nobody else can see this.

Bm7
Uh, so watch and learn, I won't show you twice.

Em7
Head to toe, oo, baby, roll me right, ___ yeah.

But if I share my secret, you're gonna have to keep it.

Nobody else can see this, hey, hey, hey, yeah.

N.C.
Male: And it goes like this.

Chorus 3

                                      Bm7
Both: Take me by the tongue and I'll know you.

Kiss me 'til you're drunk and I'll show you
        Em7
All the moves like Jagger.

I've got the moves like Jagger.

I've got the moves like Jagger.
Bm7
  I don't need to try to control you.

Look into my eyes and I'll own you
        Em7
With the moves like Jagger.

I've got the moves like Jagger.

I've got the moves like Jagger.

Outro |**Bm7** | N.C.

Need You Now

Words and Music by Hillary Scott,
Charles Kelley, Dave Haywood and
Josh Kear

Melody:

Pic-ture per-fect mem-'ries   scat-tered all a-round

F   Am   Fmaj7 Fmaj7sus2 Asus2   Asus4   C   Em   G   Gsus4

2 1   2   2413   413   2 3   23   3   3421   132   134

Intro
| F | | Am | | |
| Fmaj7 | | Am | | |

Verse 1

                   Fmaj7   **Am**
Female: Picture perfect mem'ries scattered all around the floor.

    Fmaj7   **Am**
Reachin' for the phone 'cause I can't fight it anymore.

Pre-Chorus 1

                                Fmaj7sus2   **Am** **Asus2**
Male & Female: And I won - der if I ever cross your mind.

   Asus4 **Am**   **Fmaj7sus2**
           For me it hap - pens all the time.

Chorus 1

                          C   **Em**
Both: It's a quarter after one, I'm all alone and I need ____ you now.

                   C   **Em**
Said ____ I wouldn't call but I lost all control and I need ____ you now.

                  Fmaj7sus2
And I don't ____ know how I can do without.

I just need you now.

Interlude 1
| Fmaj7 | | Am | | |

Verse 2

                    Fmaj7   Am
Male: An - other shot of whiskey, can't stop lookin' at the door,

        Fmaj7   Am
Wish - ing you'd come sweeping in the way you did before.

Pre-Chorus 1

                            Fmaj7   Am
Male & Female: And I won - der if I ever cross your mind.

                     Fmaj7
Male: For me it hap - pens all the time.

Chorus 2

                            C
Both: It's a quarter after one, I'm a little drunk

                Em
And I need ___ you now.

                 C
Said ___ I wouldn't call but I lost all control

                Em
And I need ___ you now.

                    Fmaj7sus2
And I don't ___ know how I can do without.

I just need you now.

Guitar Solo

  |Am G   C | |Fmaj7 |Gsus4 G |
                                                        Male: Whoa, whoa.

  |Am G   C | |Fmaj7sus2 |Gsus4 |

Pre-Chorus 3

                    Fmaj7sus2   Am Gsus4
Both: Yes, I'd rather hurt and then feel nothing at all.

Chorus 3

                          C
Female: It's a quarter after one, I'm all alone

                Em
And I need ___ you now.

                      C
Male: And I said ___ I wouldn't call but I'm a little drunk

                Em
And I need ___ you now.

                    Fmaj7sus2
Both: And I don't ___ know how I can do without.

                                C   Em   C   Em
I just need you now. ___   I just need you now.

C Em   C   Em C Em
        Female: Oh, baby, I need you now.

One More Night

Words and Music by Adam Levine,
Johan Schuster and Max Martin

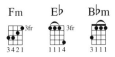

Fm	Eb	Bbm
3421	1114	3111

Intro

    Fm   Eb Bbm
Ooh, ooh, ooh, ooh, ooh, ooh, ooh.

    Fm
Ooh, ooh, ooh, ooh, ooh, ooh, ooh.

Verse 1

    Eb Bbm   Fm
          You and I go hard at each other

        Eb   Bbm
Like we're going to war.

        Fm
You and I go rough, we keep throwing things

        Eb   Bbm
And slamming the doors.

        Fm
You and I get so damn dysfunctional,

    Eb   Bbm
We start keeping score.

        Fm
You and I get sick and I know

        Eb   Bbm
That we can't do this no more, ___ yeah.

Pre-Chorus 1

Fm
But baby, there you go again, there you go again,

E♭   B♭m
Making me love you.

   Fm
Yeah, I stopped using my head, using my head,

E♭   B♭m
Let it all go, ooh.

   Fm
Got you stuck on my body, on my body,

E♭ B♭m
Like a tattoo.

   Fm
And now I'm feeling stupid, feeling stupid

E♭   B♭m
Crawling back you.

Chorus 1

   Fm   E♭
So I cross my heart and I hope to die

B♭m Fm   E♭
 That I'll only stay with you one more night.

B♭m Fm   E♭
 And I know I said it a million times

B♭m Fm   E♭
 But I'll only stay with you one more night.

Verse 2

N.C.   Fm
   Try to tell you "no," but my body keeps on

Eb   Bbm
Telling you, "yes."

                Fm
Try to tell you, "stop," but your lipstick got me

Eb   Bbm
So out of breath.

                Eb
I'll be waking up in the morning prob'bly

Eb   Bbm
Hating myself.

                Eb
I'll be waking up feeling satisfied

     Eb   Bbm
But guilty as hell, ___ yeah.

Pre-Chorus 2   *Repeat Pre-Chorus 1*

Chorus 2   *Repeat Chorus 1*

Bridge

 Fm
(Ooh, ooh, ooh, ooh, ooh, ooh, ooh.)

Eb   Bbm
  Yeah, baby, give me one more night.

 Fm
(Ooh, ooh, ooh, ooh, ooh, ooh, ooh.)

Eb
  Yeah, baby, give me

Bbm   Fm
One more night. __   Whoa,   yeah.
             (Ooh, ooh, ooh, ooh, ooh, ooh, ooh.)

Eb   Bbm   Fm   Eb Bbm
  Yeah, baby, give me one more night. ___ Oh, yeah.

Pre-Chorus 3

Fm
Oh, baby, there you go again, there you go again,

E♭   B♭m
Making me love you.

Fm
Yeah, I stopped using my head, using my head,

E♭   B♭m
Let it all go.

Fm
Got you stuck on my body, on my body,

E♭   B♭m
Like a tattoo.

Fm   E♭ B♭m
Yeah, ___ yeah, yeah, yeah.

Chorus 3

Fm   E♭ B♭m
‖: So I cross my heart and I hope to die

Fm   E♭ B♭m
That I'll only stay with you one more night.

Fm   E♭ B♭m
And I know I said it a million times

Fm   E♭ B♭m
But I'll only stay with you one more night.   :‖

Fm N.C.
Spoken: *I don't know, whatever.*

Rolling in the Deep

Words and Music by Adele Adkins
and Paul Epworth

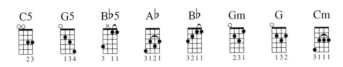

There's a   fi - re   start-ing in my __ heart,

C5   G5   Bb5   Ab   Bb   Gm   G   Cm

Intro
| C5 | | ‖

Verse 1

C5   G5
There's a fire start-ing in my heart,

    Bb5   G5   Bb5
Reach-ing a fever pitch and it's bring-ing me out the dark.

C5   G5
Finally I can see you crystal clear,

    Bb5   G5   Bb5
Go ahead and sell me out and I'll lay your shit bare.

Verse 2

C5   G5
See how I'll leave with every__ piece of you,

    Bb5   G5   Bb5
Don't underestimate the things that I will do.

C5   G5
There's a fire start-ing in my heart,

    Bb5   G5   Bb5
Reach-ing a fever pitch and it's bring-ing me out the dark.

Pre-Chorus 1

    Ab   Bb   Gm
  The scars of your love remind me of us,

                Ab   Bb Ab
They keep me thinking that we almost had it   all.

         Bb   Gm
The scars of your love, they leave me breathless;

        G
I can't help feeling…

Chorus 1

                Cm   Bb
We could have had it all, (You're gonna wish you never had met me.)

                Ab
Rolling in the deep. (Tears are gonna fall, rolling in the deep.)

     Bb   Cm   Bb   Ab   Bb
You had my heart in-side your hand,__ and you played it to the beat.

Verse 3

C5   G5
Baby, I have no sto-ry to be told,

      Bb5   G5   Bb5
But I've heard one on you and I'm gonna make your head burn.

C5   G5
Think of me in the depths of your despair,

      Bb5   G5   Bb5
Mak-ing a home down there as mine sure won't be shared.

Pre-Chorus 2   *Repeat Pre-Chorus 1*

Chorus 2   *Repeat Chorus 1*

Chorus 3

                Ab Bb
Could have had it all._____

            Cm   Bb
Rolling in the deep._____

               Ab   Bb
You had my heart in-side your hand, but you played__ it with a beating.

Verse 4

N.C.
   Throw your soul through every open door,

Count your blessings to find what you look for.

Cm
Turn my sorrow into treasured gold.

Pay me back in kind and reap just what you sow.

Outro-Chorus

      Cm   Bb
‖: (You're gonna wish you never had met me.

Ab   Bb
Tears are gonna fall, rolling in the deep). :‖ *Play 5 times*

Cm   Bb   *w/ lead vocal ad lib.*
(You're gonna wish you never had met me.)

        Ab
But you played it, you played it, you played it,

        Bb   Cm
You played__ it to the beat.

Some Nights

Words and Music by Jeff Bhasker,
Andrew Dost, Jack Antonoff
and Nate Ruess

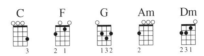

Some nights I stay — up   cash-in' in my bad   luck, —

Verse 1

   C   F   C
Some nights I stay up cashin' in my bad luck,

F   C   G
Some nights I call it a draw.

C   F   C
Some nights I wish that my lips could build a castle,

F   C   G
Some nights I wish they'd just fall off.

       F   C   F   C
But I still wake up, I still see your ghost.

             F   C   G
Oh Lord, I'm still not sure what I stand for, oh.

         F   C   F   C
Whoa, ___ what do I stand for?   What do I stand for?

Am   G
Most nights, I don't know

Interlude 1

     F   C   F C   F C   G
Any - More, __ oh, oh, __ oh, oh, __ oh.

F   C   F C   F C   G
Oh, __ oh, oh, __ oh, oh, __ oh.

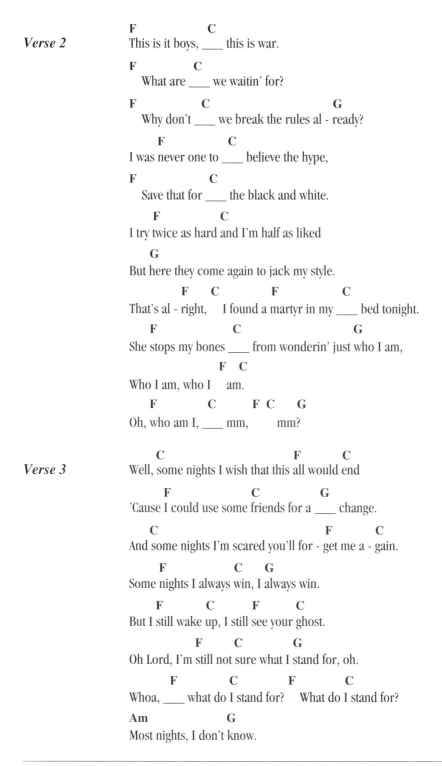

Verse 2

F   C
This is it boys, ____ this is war.

F   C
 What are ____ we waitin' for?

F   C   G
 Why don't ____ we break the rules al - ready?

    F   C
I was never one to ____ believe the hype,

F   C
 Save that for ____ the black and white.

    F   C
I try twice as hard and I'm half as liked

    G
But here they come again to jack my style.

       F C   F   C
That's al - right, I found a martyr in my ____ bed tonight.

    F   C   G
She stops my bones ____ from wonderin' just who I am,

           F C
Who I am, who I am.

     F   C   F C   G
Oh, who am I, ____ mm,   mm?

Verse 3

     C   F   C
Well, some nights I wish that this all would end

     F   C   G
'Cause I could use some friends for a ____ change.

     C   F   C
And some nights I'm scared you'll for - get me a - gain.

     F   C G
Some nights I always win, I always win.

     F   C   F   C
But I still wake up, I still see your ghost.

        F   C   G
Oh Lord, I'm still not sure what I stand for, oh.

      F   C   F   C
Whoa, ____ what do I stand for? What do I stand for?

Am   G
Most nights, I don't know.

Bridge

                   F
(Oh, come on.) __ *Spoken: So this is it.*

C
   I sold my soul for this.

G
   Washed my hands of that for this?
          (Ooh,   na,   na.)

   I miss my mom and dad for this?
          (ooh,   na,   na.)

    F
No, when I see stars, when I see,

C
   When I see stars, that's all they are.
         (Ooh, na   na.   Come on.)

         G
When I hear __ songs,
         (Ooh, na, na.)

They sound like this one, so come on.
         (Ooh, na,   na.)

F   **C**   **G**
  Oh, come on. __ Oh, come on. __ Oh, come on.

Verse 4

```
              F               C
Well, that is it guys, ____ that is all.
F            C
Five minutes in and I'm bored again.
F              C               G
Ten years of this, I'm not sure if any - body understands.
      F              C
This one is not for ____ the folks at home.
F              C
Sorry to leave Mom, I had to go.
F              C                    G
   Who the fuck wants to die alone all dried up in the desert sun?
              F                          C
My heart is breaking for my sister and the con that she call "love."
      G                        Dm
When I look into my nephew's eyes,     man, you wouldn't believe
F                        Dm                  G
   The most amazing things     that can come from
```

Some terrible

Interlude 2

```
F    C F   C F   C   G
lies. _____ Ah, __ oh.
F   C     F  C F   C    G
Ah, ____ ah, ____   ah, __ ah.
F   C    F  C     F   C   G
Oh, __oh, oh, __ oh, oh, __ oh.
F   C    F  C     F   C   G
Oh, __oh, oh, __ oh, oh, __ oh.
```

Outro

```
F                      C
   The other night ____ you wouldn't believe
              F           C
The dream ____ I just had about you and me.
F              C                G
   I called you up but we both agree.
     F    C                     F  C
‖:   It's for the best you didn't lis - ten.
F    C                    G
   It's for the best we get our dis - tance, oh.  :‖ *Repeat and fade*
```

Stereo Hearts

Words and Music by Travis McCoy,
Adam Levine, Brandon Lowry, Daniel Omelio,
Benjamin Levin and Ammar Malik

Melody:

My heart's a ster - e - o, ____

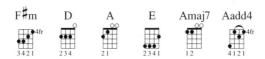

F#m   D   A   E   Amaj7 Aadd4

Chorus 1

F#m D   A   E   F#m

My heart's a stereo, ____ it beats for you, ____ so listen close.

             D   A   E

Hear my thoughts ____ in ev'ry no - o - ote.

F#m   D   A   E   F#m

Make me your radio, ____ and turn me up ____ when you feel low.

             D   A

This melody ____ was meant for you,

             E

Just sing along ____ to my stereo. *Spoken: Gym Class Heroes, Ravi.*

Verse 1

N.C.(F#m)
If I was just another dusty record on the shelf,

(D) (A)
Would you blow me off and play me like ev'rybody else?

(E) (F#m)
If I ask you to scratch my back, can you manage that?

(D) (A)
Like yeah (scratched) check it, Travie, I can handle that.

(E) (F#m)
Furthermore, I apolo - gize for any skippin' tracks.

(D) (A)
This is the last girl that played me, left a couple cracks.

(E) (F#m)
I used to used to used to used to, now I'm over that.

(D) (A)
'Cause holdin' grudges over love is ancient artifacts.

(E) (F#m)
If I could only find a note to make you understand.

(D) (A)
I sing it softly in your ear and grab you by the hands.

(E) (F#m)
Just keep me stuck inside your head, like your fav'rite tune.

(D) (A) (E)
And know my heart's a stere - o that only plays for you.

Chorus 2

F#m D A E F#m
My heart's a stereo, ___ it beats for you, ___ so listen close.

D A E
Hear my thoughts ___ in ev'ry no - o - ote.

F#m D A E F#m
Make me your radio, ___ and turn me up ___ when you feel low.

D A
This melody ___ was meant for you,

E N.C.
Just sing a - long ___ to my stereo.

A Amaj7 Aadd4
Oh, oh, oh, oh, oh, oh, oh, oh, oh, oh, oh, oh.

D E N.C.
So sing a - long to my stere - o. *Let's go.*

Verse 2

                             N.C.(F♯m)
If I was an old school, fifty pound boombox

(D)   **(A)**
Would you hold me on your shoulder, wherever you walk?

(E)   **(F♯m)**
Would you turn my volume up in front of the cops

(D)   **(A)**
And crank it higher ev'ry - time they told you to stop?

(E)   **(F♯m)**
And all I ask is that you don't get mad at me

(D)   **(A)**
When you have to purchase mad D batteries.

(E)   **(F♯m)**
Appreciate ev'ry mixtape your friends make

(D)   **(A)**
You never know we come and go like we're on the interstate.

(E)   **(F♯m)**
I think I fin'lly found a note that make you understand.

(D)   **(A)**
If you can hear this, sing a - long and take me by the hands.

(E)   **(F♯m)**
Just keep me stuck inside your head, like your fav'rite tune.

(D)   **(A)**   **(E)**
You know my hearts a stere - o that only plays for you.

Chorus 3

F#m D   A   E   F#m
  My heart's a stereo, ___ it beats for you, ___ so listen close.

           D   A   E
Hear my thoughts ___ in ev'ry no - o - ote.

F#m D   A   E   F#m
  Make me your radio, ___ and turn me up ___ when you feel low.

        D   A
This melody ___ was meant for you,

      E N.C.
Just sing a - long ___ to my stereo.

A   Amaj7   Aadd4
Oh, oh, oh, oh, oh, oh, oh, oh, oh, oh, oh, oh.

D   E   F#m
  So sing a - long to my stere - o

Verse 3

      D   A   E
I only pray you'll never leave me behind,

F#m   D   A   E
  Because good music can be so hard to find.

F#m   D   A   E
  I'll take your hand and pull it closer to mine.

F#m   D   A   F#m
  Thought love was dead, but now you're changing my mind.

Chorus 4

F#m D   A   E   F#m
  My heart's a stereo, ___ it beats for you, ___ so listen close.

           D   A   E
Hear my thoughts ___ in ev'ry note, ___ oh, oh.

F#m D   A   E   F#m
  Make me your radio, ___ and turn me up ___ when you feel low.

        D   A
This melody ___ was meant for you,

      E N.C.
Just sing a - long ___ to my stereo.

A   Amaj7   Aadd4
Oh, oh, oh, oh, oh, oh, oh, oh, oh, oh, oh, oh.

D   E   A N.C.
  So sing a - long to my stere - o. *Yeah!*

Stronger
(What Doesn't Kill You)

Words and Music by Greg Kurstin,
Jorgen Elofsson, David Gamson
and Alexandra Tamposi

You know the bed feels warm - er _____

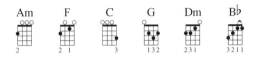

Intro | Am | F | C | G |

Verse 1

Am   F
   You know the bed feels warm - er

C   G
Sleepin' here alone.

Am   F
   You know I dream in col - or

   C   G
And do the things I want.

Am   F
   You think you got the best of me,   think you had the last laugh.

C   G
   Bet you think that ev'rything good is gone.

Am   F
   Think you left me broken down,   think that I'd come runnin' back.

C   G
   Baby, you don't know me 'cause you're dead wrong.

Chorus 1

N.C.   **Am**
What doesn't kill you makes you stronger,

          F
Stand a little taller.

                 C
Doesn't mean I'm lonely when I'm alone.

G   **Am**
What doesn't kill you makes a fighter,

          F
Footsteps even lighter.

                 C
Doesn't mean I'm over 'cause you're gone.

G   **Am**
What doesn't kill you makes you   stronger,

       F   **C**
Strong - er, just me, myself and I.

G   **Am**
What doesn't kill you makes you stronger,

          F
Stand a little taller.

                 C   **G**
Doesn't mean I'm lonely when I'm alone.

Verse 2

Am   **F**   **C**   **G**
You heard that I was start - ing over with someone new.

Am   **F**   **C**   **G**
They told you I was a mov - in' on and over you.

Am   **F**
You didn't think that I'd come back,   I'd come back swingin'.

C   **N.C.**
You tried to break me. But you see…

Chorus 2   *Repeat Chorus 1*

Bridge

Dm
Thanks to you I got a new thing started,
B♭
Thanks to you I'm not the broken hearted.
Am
Thanks to you I'm fin'lly thinkin' 'bout me.
   F   Am
You know in the end, the day I left was just a my begin - ning.
F   C
In the end,

Chorus 3

N.C.   Am
What doesn't kill you makes you stronger,
                    F
Stand a little taller.
                        C
Doesn't mean I'm lonely when I'm alone.
G   Am
What doesn't kill you makes a fighter,
                      F
Footsteps even lighter.
                        C
Doesn't mean I'm over 'cause you're gone.
G   Am
What doesn't kill you makes you   stronger,
            F   C
Strong - er, just me, myself and I.
G   Am
What doesn't kill you makes you stronger,
                    F
Stand a little taller.
                       C   G
Doesn't mean I'm lonely when I'm alone.
                        Am
What doesn't kill you makes you   stronger,
            F   C
Strong - er, just me, myself and I.
G   Am
What doesn't kill you makes you stronger,
                    F
Stand a little taller.
                       C   G   Am F C G
Doesn't mean I'm lonely when I'm alone, ___ alone.

Teenage Dream

Words and Music by Katy Perry,
Bonnie McKee, Lukasz Gottwald,
Max Martin and Benjamin Levin

You think I'm pret-ty with-out an-y make-up on, ___

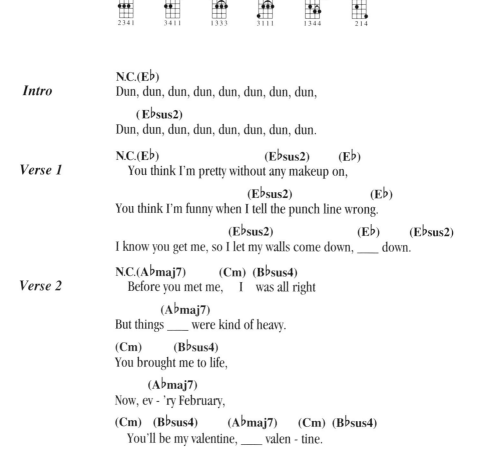

Intro

N.C.(E♭)
Dun, dun, dun, dun, dun, dun, dun, dun,

(E♭sus2)
Dun, dun, dun, dun, dun, dun, dun, dun.

Verse 1

N.C.(E♭)   (E♭sus2)   (E♭)
   You think I'm pretty without any makeup on,

                         (E♭sus2)   (E♭)
You think I'm funny when I tell the punch line wrong.

                      (E♭sus2)   (E♭)   (E♭sus2)
I know you get me, so I let my walls come down, ___ down.

Verse 2

N.C.(A♭maj7)   (Cm) (B♭sus4)
   Before you met me,   I   was all right

         (A♭maj7)
But things ___ were kind of heavy.

(Cm)   (B♭sus4)
You brought me to life,

       (A♭maj7)
Now, ev - 'ry February,

(Cm) (B♭sus4)   (A♭maj7)   (Cm) (B♭sus4)
   You'll be my valentine, ___ valen - tine.

Pre-Chorus 1

N.C.(A♭maj7) (Cm) (B♭sus4)
Let's go all the   way   tonight,

(A♭maj7) (Cm) (B♭sus4)
No regrets, ____ just love.

(A♭maj7) (Cm) (B♭sus4)
We can dance un - til   we die,

(A♭maj7)   (Cm) (B♭sus4)
You and I ____ will be young forever.

Chorus 1

N.C.(A♭maj7) (Cm) (B♭sus4)
You make me _____ feel

(A♭maj7)   (Cm)
Like I'm living a teenage dream,

(B♭sus4)   (A♭maj7) (Cm)
The way you turn me on. I can't sleep.

(B♭sus4)   (A♭maj7)
Let's run away and don't ever look back,

(Cm)   (B♭sus4)
Don't ____ ev - er look back.

(A♭maj7)   (Cm) (B♭sus4)
My heart stops ____   when you look at me.

(A♭maj7)   (Cm) (B♭sus4)
Just one touch, ____   now, baby,

(A♭maj7) (Cm)
I believe this is real.

(B♭sus4)   (A♭maj7)
So take a chance and don't ever look back,

(Cm)   (B♭sus4)
Don't ____ ev - er look back.

Verse 3

N.C.(A♭maj7)   (Cm) (B♭sus4)
    We drove to Cali   and got drunk on the beach,

(A♭maj7)   (Cm) (B♭sus4)
  Got a motel and built a fort out of sheets.

(A♭maj7)   (Cm) (B♭sus4)
  I fin'lly found you,   my missing puzzle piece.

(A♭maj7) (Cm) (B♭sus4)
  I'm com - plete.

Pre-Chorus 2   *Repeat Pre-Chorus 1*

Chorus 2   *Repeat Chorus 1*

Verse 4

           N.C.(A♭maj7) (Cm) (B♭sus4)
I'm a get your heart racing in my skin - tight jeans,

        (A♭maj7)   (Cm)
Be your teenage dream to - night.

(B♭sus4)   (A♭maj7)   (Cm) (B♭sus4)
  Let you put your hands on me in my skin - tight jeans,

        (A♭maj7)   (Cm) (E♭maj9)
Be your teenage dream to - night. Ooh, ooh, ooh, ah.

Interlude

N.C.(A♭maj7) (Cm) (B♭sus4)
  Ooh,   ooh, ooh.

(A♭maj7) (Cm) (B♭sus4)
Oh,   ah,   ah.

Chorus 3   *Repeat Chorus 1*

Verse 5

           N.C.(A♭maj7) (Cm) (B♭sus4)
I'm a get your heart racing in my skin - tight jeans,

        (A♭maj7)   (Cm) (B♭sus4)
Be your teenage dream to - night.

N.C.
Let you put your hands on me in my skintight jeans,

Be your teenage dream tonight.

Titanium

Words and Music by David Guetta,
Sia Furler, Giorgio Tuinfort
and Nik Van De Wall

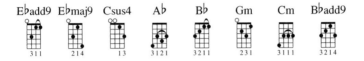

| Ebadd9 | Ebmaj9 | Csus4 | Ab | Bb | Gm | Cm | Bbadd9 |

Intro ‖: Ebadd9 │ Ebmaj9 │ Csus4 │ │ :‖

Verse 1

Ebadd9   Ebmaj9   Csus4
You shout it out, ___ but I ___ can't hear a word you say.

Ebadd9   Csus4
I'm talking loud, not saying much.

Ebadd9   Ebmaj9   Csus4
I'm criticized, ___ but all ___ your bullets ricochet.

Ebadd9   Csus4
You shoot me down, but I get up.

Chorus 1

A♭   B♭   Gm
I'm bulletproof, ___ nothing to lose.

    Cm   A♭
Fire away, ___ fire away.

    B♭   Gm
Ricochet, ___ you take your aim,

    Cm   A♭
Fire away, ___ fire away.

      B♭   Gm
You shoot me down, ___ but I won't fall,

   Cm A♭
I am tita - nium.

      B♭   Gm
You shoot me down, ___ but I won't fall,

   Cm A♭ B♭add9 Gm Cm A♭ B♭add9 Gm Cm
I am tita - nium.

Verse 2

E♭add9   E♭maj9   Csus4
Cut me down, ___ but it's you ___ who have further to fall.

E♭add9   Csus4
Mm, ghost town and haunted love.

E♭add9   E♭maj9 Csus4
Raise your voice, ___ sticks ___ and stones may break my bones.

E♭add9   Csus4
Talking loud, not saying much.

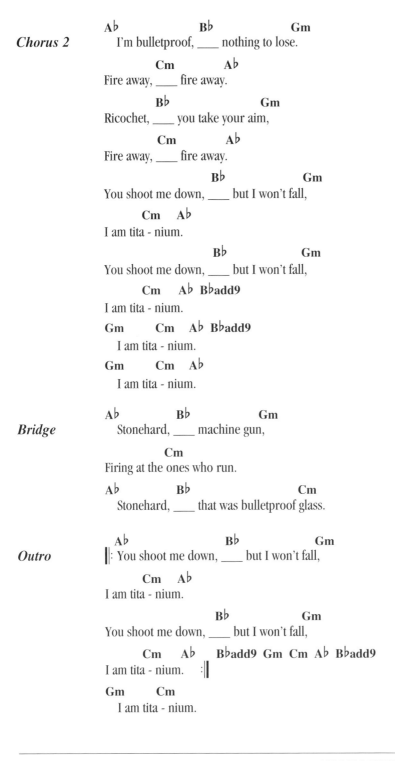

Chorus 2

Ab   Bb   Gm
I'm bulletproof, ___ nothing to lose.

        Cm   Ab
Fire away, ___ fire away.

        Bb   Gm
Ricochet, ___ you take your aim,

        Cm   Ab
Fire away, ___ fire away.

               Bb   Gm
You shoot me down, ___ but I won't fall,

      Cm   Ab
I am tita - nium.

               Bb   Gm
You shoot me down, ___ but I won't fall,

      Cm   Ab Bbadd9
I am tita - nium.

Gm   Cm   Ab Bbadd9
  I am tita - nium.

Gm   Cm   Ab
  I am tita - nium.

Bridge

Ab   Bb   Gm
Stonehard, ___ machine gun,

        Cm
Firing at the ones who run.

Ab   Bb   Cm
Stonehard, ___ that was bulletproof glass.

Outro

    Ab   Bb   Gm
‖: You shoot me down, ___ but I won't fall,

      Cm   Ab
I am tita - nium.

              Bb   Gm
You shoot me down, ___ but I won't fall,

      Cm   Ab   Bbadd9 Gm Cm Ab Bbadd9
I am tita - nium.   :‖

Gm   Cm
  I am tita - nium.

Too Close

Words and Music by
Alex Claire and Jim Duguid

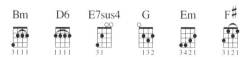

You know I'm not one   to break ___ prom-is - es.

Bm   D6   E7sus4   G   Em   F♯

3111   1111   31   132   3421   3121

Intro ‖: Bm |D6 |E7sus4 |G :‖ *Play 4 times*

Verse 1

Bm   D6   Em   G F♯
You know I'm not one   to break ___ promises.

Bm   D6   Em G F♯
I don't wanna hurt ___ you but I need to breathe.

Bm   D6   Em   G F♯
At the end of it all, ___ you're still my best ___ friend.

Bm   D6   Em G F♯
But there's something inside ___ that I need to release.

Bm   D6
Which way is right? Which way is wrong?

Em   G   F♯
How do I say that I need ___ to move ___ on?

Bm   D6   Em G F♯
You know we're head - ing sep'rate ways.

Chorus 1

    Bm   D6   Em   G F♯

And it feels like I am just too close to love ___ you.

Bm   D6   Em G F♯

There's nothing I ___ can really say.

Bm   D6

I can't lie no more.   I can't hide no more.

Em   G F♯

Got to be true to myself.

     Bm   D6   Em

And it feels like I am just too close to love ___ you.

G   F♯

So I'll be on my way.

Interlude   ‖: Bm | D6 | Em | G F♯ :‖

Verse 2

Bm   D6   Em G F♯

You've given me more ___ than I can re - turn.

Bm   D6   Em G F♯

Yet there's, oh, so much ___ that you deserve.

Bm   D6

Nothing to say. Nothing to do.

  Em   G   F♯

I've nothing to give, I must live ___ without ___ you.

Bm   D6   Em G F♯

You know we're head - ing sep'rate ways.

Chorus 2

N.C.   **Em**   **G F♯**
And it feels like I am just too close to love ___ you.

Bm   **D6**   **Em G F♯**
  There's nothing I ___ can really say.

Bm   **D6**
  I can't lie no more.   I can't hide no more.

Em   **G F♯**
  Got to be true to myself.

      Bm   **D6**   **Em**
And it feels like I am just too close to love ___ you.

G   **F♯**   **Bm D6 Em**
  So I'll be on my way.

G   **Bm D6 Em G**
  So I'll be on my way.

Outro-Chorus

      Bm   **D6**   **Em**   **G F♯**
And it feels like I am just too close to love ___ you.

Bm   **D6**   **Em G F♯**
  There's nothing I ___ can really say.

Bm   **D6**
  I can't lie no more.   I can't hide no more.

E7sus4   **G F♯**
  Got to be true to myself.

      Bm   **D6**   **Em**
And it feels like I am just too close to love ___ you.

G   **F♯**   **Bm D6 E7sus4**
  So I'll be on my way.

G   **Bm D6 E7sus4**
  So I'll be on my way.

G   **Bm**
  So I'll be on my way.

We Are Never Ever Getting Back Together

Words and Music by Taylor Swift,
Shellback and Max Martin

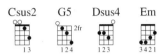

I re-mem-ber when we broke _ up the first time.

Csus2   G5   Dsus4   Em

Intro
| Csus2 G5 | Dsus4 Em |

Verse 1

Csus2   G5
I remember when we broke up the first time.

Dsus4   Em
Saying, "This is it, I've had e - nough."

      Csus2   G5
'Cause like, we hadn't seen each other in a month

     Dsus4   Em
When you said you needed space. *Spoken: What?*

Csus2   G5
Then you come around again and say,

     Dsus4   Em
"Baby, I miss you and I swear I'm gonna change." *Spoken: "Trust me."*

    Csus2   G5
Re - member how that lasted for a day.

     Dsus4
I say, "I hate you." We break up.

    Em
You call me, *Spoken: "I love you."*

Pre-Chorus 1

Csus2 G5
Oo,   oo, oo,

     Dsus4   Em
We called it off again _____ last night.

     Csus2 G5
But oo,   oo, oo,

Dsus4   Em
This time I'm telling you, I'm telling you

Chorus 1

Csus2 G5   Dsus4
We are never, ever, ever,

     Em   D5
Getting back to - gether.

Csus2 G5   Dsus4
We are never, ever, ever,

     Em   D5
Getting back to - gether.

Csus2   G5
You go talk to your _____ friends,

      Dsus4   Em
Talk to my _____ friends, talk to me.

D5   Csus2 G5   Dsus4
  But we are never, ever, ever, _____ ever

     N.C.   Csus2
Getting back to - gether.

     G5   Dsus4 Em
Spoken: Like, ever.

Verse 2

Csus2   G5
I'm really gonna miss you picking fights.

   Dsus4   Em
And me, falling for it, screaming that I'm right.

      Csus2   G5
And you would hide away and find your peace of mind with some

    Dsus4   Em
Spoken: Indie record that's much cooler than mine.

Pre-Chorus 2

Csus2 G5
Oo,   oo, oo,

  Dsus4   Em
You called me up again ___ tonight.

   Csus2 G5
But oo,   oo, oo,

Dsus4   Em
This time I'm telling you, I'm telling you

Chorus 2

Csus2 G5   Dsus4
We are never, ever, ever,

     Em   D5
Getting back to - gether.

Csus2 G5   Dsus4
We are never, ever, ever,

     Em   D5
Getting back to - gether.

Csus2   G5
You go talk to your ___ friends,

     Dsus4   Em
Talk to my ___ friends, talk to me.

D5   Csus2 G5   Dsus4
  But we are never, ever, ever, ___ ever

        N.C.   Csus2
Getting back to - gether.

G5   Dsus4 Em
  Yeah.   Yeah.

Csus2 G5   Dsus4   Em D5
          Yeah,   oh, oh.

Bridge

Csus2   G5   Dsus4   Em
I used to think ___ that we ___ were for - ever, ever.

  Csus2   G5 Dsus4   Em
And I used to say ___ never say nev - er.

Csus2   G5   Dsus4
So he calls me up, and he's like "I still love you."

         Em
And I'm like,   I'm just, I mean,

  Csus2   G5
"This is exhausting, you know.

                 Dsus4   N.C.
Like, we are never getting back ___ together, like ever."

Outro-Chorus

Csus2 G5   **Dsus4**
No, we are never, ever, ever,

      Em   **D5**
Getting back to - gether.

Csus2 G5   **Dsus4**
We are never, ever, ever,

      Em   **D5**
Getting back to - gether.

Csus2   **G5**
You go talk to your ___ friends,

      Dsus4   **Em**
Talk to my ___ friends, talk to me.

D5   **Csus2 G5**   **Dsus4**
  But we are never, ever, ever, ___ ever

Em   **D5**   **Csus2 G5**
  Getting back to - gether.

Dsus4   **Em**   **D5**
  No. (Getting back to - gether.)

Csus2 G5 Dsus4   **Em**   **D5**
We   oh, getting back to - gether.

Csus2   **G5**
You go talk to your ___ friends,

      Dsus4   **Em**
Talk to my ___ friends, talk to me.

D5   **Csus2 G5**   **Dsus4**
  But we are never, ever, ever, ___ ever

      N.C.
Getting back together.

What the Hell

Words and Music by
Avril Lavigne, Max Martin
and Johan Schuster

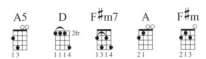

A5   D   F#m7   A   F#m

Intro |A5 |D |F#m7 | D |

Verse 1
A   D   F#m
You say that I'm messing with your head.

                    D
(Yeah, yeah, yeah, ___ yeah.)

A   D   F#m
All 'cause I was making out with your friend.

                    D
(Yeah, yeah, yeah, ___ yeah.)

A   D   F#m
Love hurts whether it's right or wrong.

                    D
(Yeah, yeah, yeah, ___ yeah.)

  A   D   F#m
I can't stop 'cause I'm having too much fun.

                    D
(Yeah, yeah, yeah, ___ yeah.)

Chorus 1

     A   D   F#m
You're on your knees, begging, "Please, stay with me."

D   A   D   F#m D
   But, honestly, I just need to be a little crazy.

A   D
All my life I've been good,

      F#m   D
But now I'm thinking what the hell?

A   D
All I want is to mess around,

    F#m   D
And I don't really care a - bout

A   D
  If you love me,   if you hate me.

F#m   D
  You can't save me, baby, ba - by.

A   D
All my life I've been good,

      F#m   D
But now, whoa, what the hell?

A5   D   F#m7   D
What?   What?   What? What the hell?

Verse 2

     A   D   F#m
So what if I go out on a million dates?

                 D
(Yeah, yeah, yeah, ___ yeah.)

       A   D   F#m
You never call or listen to me anyway.

                 D
(Yeah, yeah, yeah, ___ yeah.)

       A   D   F#m
I'd rather rage than sit around and wait all day.

                 D
(Yeah, yeah, yeah, ___ yeah.)

       A   D   F#m   D
Don't get me wrong, I just need some time to play, ___ yay.

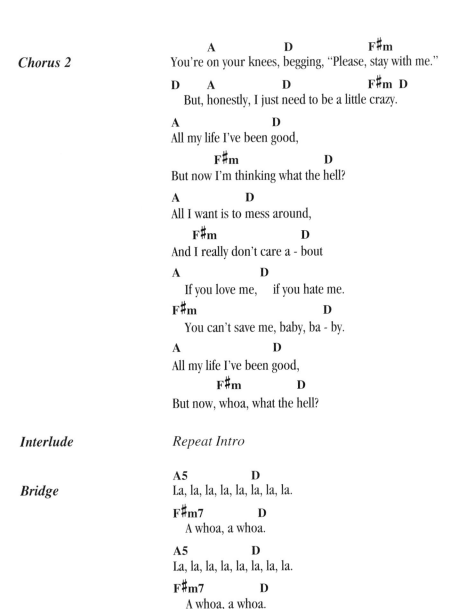

Chorus 2

        A   **D**   **F#m**
You're on your knees, begging, "Please, stay with me."

D   **A**   **D**   **F#m** **D**
  But, honestly, I just need to be a little crazy.

A   **D**
All my life I've been good,

     F#m   **D**
But now I'm thinking what the hell?

A   **D**
All I want is to mess around,

    F#m   **D**
And I really don't care a - bout

A   **D**
  If you love me,   if you hate me.

F#m   **D**
  You can't save me, baby, ba - by.

A   **D**
All my life I've been good,

     F#m   **D**
But now, whoa, what the hell?

Interlude   *Repeat Intro*

Bridge

A5   **D**
La, la, la, la, la, la, la, la.

F#m7   **D**
  A whoa, a whoa.

A5   **D**
La, la, la, la, la, la, la, la.

F#m7   **D**
  A whoa, a whoa.

Verse 3

```
A        D                      F♯m
You say that I'm messing with a your head.
              D        A
Boy, I like messing in a your bed.
        D                   F♯m
Yeah, I am messing with a your head
                  D     A
When I'm messing with you in bed.
```

Chorus 3

```
A              D
All my life I've been good,
      F♯m              D
But now I'm thinking what the hell?
A         D
All I want is to mess around,
      F♯m          D
And I really don't care a - bout…
A              D
All my life I've been good,
      F♯m              D
And now I'm thinking what the hell?
A         D
All I want is to mess around,
      F♯m          D
And I really don't care a - bout
A              D
   If you love me,    if you hate me.
F♯m                   D
   You can't save me, baby, ba - by.
A              D
All my life I've been good, but now,
F♯m          D
Whoa, what the hell?
```

Outro

```
A5    D
La, la, la, la, la, la, la, la,
F♯m7          D    N.C.
La, la, la, la, la, la, la, la, la.
```

We Found Love

Words and Music by
Calvin Harris

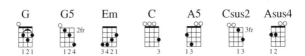

Yel-low dia - monds in the light, _____

G   G5   Em   C   A5   Csus2   Asus4

Intro   ‖: G   G5 :‖   ***Play 4 times***

Verse 1

G   G5   G   G5
   Yellow dia - monds in the light,

G   G5 G   G5
   Now we're stand - in' side by ___ side

G   G5 G   G5
   As a shad - ow crosses mine.

G   G5   G   G5 Em C G
   What it takes ___ to come a - live.

Pre-Chorus 1

A5   Em   C
   It's the way I'm feel - in',

G   A5   Em C G
I just can't ___ de - ny,

A5   Em   C   G A5
   But I've gotta let ___ it go.

Chorus 1

Em   C G   A5
We found love ___ in a hopeless place.

Em   C G A5
We found love ___ in a hopeless ___ place.

Em   C G   A5
We found love ___ in a hopeless place.

Em   C G A5
We found love ___ in a hopeless ___ place.

Interlude 1

‖: Em | | | :‖

‖: Em Csus2 |G Asus4 |Em Csus2 |G Asus4 :‖

Verse 2

Em   C   G A5
Shine a light ___ through an open door,

Em   C G A5
Love and life ___ our will de - fy.

Em   C   G   A5
Turn away ___ 'cause I need you more,

Em   C G A5 Em C G
Feel the heart - beat in my ___ mind.

Pre-Chorus 2 *Repeat Pre-Chorus 1*

Chorus 2

Em   C G   A5
We found love ____ in a hopeless place.

Em   C G A5
We found love ____ in a hopeless ____ place.

Em   C G   A5
We found love ____ in a hopeless place.

Em   C G A5 Em C
We found love ____ in a hopeless ____ place.

| Em C | Em   C | Em   C |

Verse 3

Em   C Em C
Yellow diamonds ____ in the light,

Em   C Em C
Now we're standing ____ side-by-side

Em   C Em
As a shadow ____ crosses mine.

C Em C Em C
(Mine, ____ mine, mine.)

Chorus 3   *Repeat Chorus 1*

Interlude 2   *Repeat Interlude 1*

Outro-Chorus   *Repeat Chorus 1*

UKULELE CHORD SONGBOOKS

This series features convenient 6" x 9" books with complete lyrics and chord symbols for dozens of great songs. Each song also includes chord grids at the top of every page and the first notes of the melody for easy reference.

ACOUSTIC ROCK

50 tunes: American Pie • Band on the Run • Catch the Wind • Crazy Little Thing Called Love • Daydream • Every Rose Has Its Thorn • Hallelujah • Iris • The Magic Bus • More Than Words • Only Wanna Be with You • Patience • Seven Bridges Road • The Sound of Silence • Space Oddity • Sweet Talkin' Woman • 3 AM • Wake up Little Susie • Who'll Stop the Rain • and more.
00702482 Lyrics/Chord Symbols/
          Ukulele Chord Diagrams $14.99

THE BEATLES

100 favorites: Across the Universe • Carry That Weight • Dear Prudence • Good Day Sunshine • Here Comes the Sun • If I Fell • Love Me Do • Michelle • Ob-La-Di, Ob-La-Da • Revolution • Something • Ticket to Ride • We Can Work It Out • and many more.
00703065 Lyrics/Chord Symbols/Ukulele
          Chord Diagrams $19.99

CHILDREN'S SONGS

70 classics: Alphabet Song • "C" Is for Cookie • Do-Re-Mi • I'm Popeye the Sailor Man • John Jacob Jingleheimer Schmidt • Mickey Mouse March • Oh! Susanna • Polly Wolly Doodle • Puff the Magic Dragon • The Rainbow Connection • Sing • Three Little Fishies (Itty Bitty Poo) • Won't You Be My Neighbor? • It's a Beautiful Day in the Neighborhood) • and many more.
00702473 Lyrics/Chord Symbols/
          Ukulele Chord Diagrams $14.99

CHRISTMAS CAROLS

75 favorites: Away in a Manger • Coventry Carol • Ding Dong! Merrily on High! • The First Noel • Good King Wenceslas • Hark! the Herald Angels Sing • I Saw Three Ships • Joy to the World • O Little Town of Bethlehem • Rise Up, Shepherd, and Follow • Still, Still, Still • Up on the Housetop • We Wish You a Merry Christmas • What Child Is This? • and more.
00702474 Lyrics/Chord Symbols/
          Ukulele Chord Diagrams $14.99

ISLAND SONGS

60 beach party tunes: Blue Hawaii • Day-O (The Banana Boat Song) • Don't Worry, Be Happy • Island Girl • It's Five O'Clock Somewhere • Kokomo • Lovely Hula Girl • Mele Kalikimaka • No Woman No Cry • One Paddle, Two Paddle • Red, Red Wine • Surfer Girl • Tiny Bubbles • Ukulele Lady • and many more.
00702471 Lyrics/Chord Symbols/
          Ukulele Chord Diagrams $16.99

THREE CHORD SONGS

60 songs: All Along the Watchtower • Bad Case of Loving You • Bang a Gong (Get It On) • Blue Suede Shoes • Cecilia • Do Wah Diddy Diddy • Get Back • Hound Dog • Kiss • La Bamba • Me and Bobby McGee • Not Fade Away • Rock This Town • Sweet Home Chicago • Twist and Shout • You Are My Sunshine • and more.
00702483 Lyrics/Chord Symbols/
          Ukulele Chord Diagrams $14.99

TOP HITS

31 hits: Blow Me (One Last Kiss) • Drive By • Forget You • Gangnam Style • Ho Hey • Home • Jar of Hearts • Just Dance • Little Lion Man • Moves like Jagger • Rolling in the Deep • Some Nights • Teenage Dream • We Are Never Ever Getting Back Together • and more.
00115929 Lyrics/Chord Symbols/
          Ukulele Chord Diagrams $14.99

HAL•LEONARD®
CORPORATION

777 W. BLUEMOUND RD. P.O. BOX 13819 MILWAUKEE, WI 53213

www.halleonard.com

Prices, contents, and availability subject to change without notice.

0213

HAL•LEONARD UKULELE PLAY-ALONG

Now you can play your favorite songs on your uke with great-sounding backing tracks to help you sound like a bonafide pro!

www.halleonard.com

Prices, contents, and availability subject to change without notice.

HAL•LEONARD® CORPORATION

7777 W. BLUEMOUND RD. P.O. BOX 13819 MILWAUKEE, WI 53213

0213